# A 30-DAY WEIGHT LOSS BIBLE STUDY

Dr. Maxwell Shimba

Printed in the United States of America

# TABLE OF CONTENTS

# INTRODUCTION

Welcome to "A 30 Day Weight Loss Bible Study." This book is designed to help you not only shed pounds but also grow closer to God. Each day, you will find a Bible verse, a brief devotional, and practical steps to apply biblical principles to your weight loss journey. By combining faith and fitness, you will find strength and encouragement from the Lord to achieve your goals.

Why a Bible Study for Weight Loss?

Weight loss is often seen purely as a physical challenge, but it is much more than that. It involves emotional, mental, and spiritual dimensions. Many people struggle with weight loss because they focus only on diet and exercise, neglecting the spiritual and emotional aspects. This Bible study integrates all these dimensions, providing a holistic approach to health and wellness.

God cares about every aspect of our lives, including our health. The Bible is full of wisdom on how to live a healthy and fulfilling life. By turning to Scripture, we can find guidance and encouragement to help us make better choices, stay motivated, and persevere through challenges.

The Importance of Faith in Your Journey

Faith plays a crucial role in any transformation journey. It provides the foundation for lasting change and helps you stay grounded and focused. Trusting in God's plan and relying on His strength can make a significant difference in your weight loss journey. When you commit your goals to the Lord and seek His guidance, you are more likely to succeed.

In Philippians 4:13, Paul writes, "I can do all this through him who gives me strength." This verse reminds us that we are not alone in our journey. God is with us, providing the strength and perseverance we need to overcome obstacles and achieve our goals. By integrating faith into your weight loss journey, you invite God's power into your life, making the impossible possible.

How to Use This Book

This Bible study is designed to be flexible and adaptable to your needs. Each day includes:

1. Bible Verse: A scripture that provides wisdom and encouragement for your journey.

2. Devotional: A brief reflection on the verse and its application to your weight loss journey.

3. Practical Steps: Actionable advice and steps to help you apply the principles from the devotional to your daily life.

4. Reflection Questions: Questions to help you think more deeply about the day's topic and how it applies to your journey.

5. Daily Affirmation: A positive statement to reinforce the day's lesson and keep you motivated.

You can start this study at any time and move at your own pace. Whether you go through it day by day or take a more extended period, the important thing is to engage with the material and apply it to your life. Feel free to journal your thoughts and prayers as you go along, making this study a personal and transformative experience.

Setting Your Goals

Before you begin, take some time to set clear and realistic goals for your weight loss journey. Consider both short-term and long-term goals, and write them down. Reflect on why these goals are important to you and how achieving them will impact your life. Pray over your goals, asking God for guidance and strength to pursue them.

Finding Support

Weight loss is often easier and more enjoyable with support. Consider sharing your journey with a friend, family member, or support group. Having someone to encourage you, hold you accountable, and celebrate your successes can make a significant difference. You might also consider joining a Bible study group or an online community focused on faith and fitness.

Staying Motivated

Staying motivated can be challenging, especially when progress seems slow or obstacles arise. This Bible study aims to keep you inspired and focused by providing daily doses of spiritual encouragement and practical advice. Remember that every step forward, no matter how small, is progress. Celebrate your victories and learn from your setbacks.

Prayer and Reflection

Throughout this journey, make prayer and reflection a daily practice. Spend time with God, seeking His wisdom and guidance. Reflect on your progress and adjust your goals and strategies as needed. Remember that God is with you every step of the way, providing the strength and perseverance you need.

Commitment to the Journey

Embarking on a weight loss journey is a significant commitment, but it is one that can lead to profound transformation. By integrating faith into your journey, you are setting yourself up for success not just physically, but emotionally, mentally, and spiritually as well. Trust in God's plan, rely on His strength, and stay committed to your goals.

As you begin this 30-day Bible study, remember that you are not alone. God is with you, guiding and supporting you every step of the way. Embrace this journey as an opportunity for growth and transformation. With faith, determination, and the support of this study, you can achieve your weight loss goals and experience the fullness of life that God desires for you.

Let's get started on this exciting journey together. May God bless you and empower you as you take these steps towards a healthier, more fulfilling life.

DR. MAXWELL SHIMBA

DAY 01

---

# COMMITMENT

Bible Verse:

_"Commit to the LORD whatever you do, and he will establish your plans."_ – Proverbs 16:3

Devotional:

Commitment is the foundation of success in any endeavor, especially in a weight loss journey. Proverbs 16:3 encourages us to commit whatever we do to the Lord, promising that He will establish our plans. This commitment signifies more than just a mental decision; it is an act of faith, trusting that God will guide and sustain us.

When we look at the Hebrew word for "commit" used in this verse, it is "galal," which means to roll away or roll onto. This imagery suggests that we should roll our burdens, our plans, and our concerns onto the Lord. By doing so, we acknowledge that we cannot achieve our goals by our own strength but need God's intervention.

Consider the story of Hannah in 1 Samuel 1. Hannah desperately wanted a child and committed her desire to the Lord through fervent prayer. In her commitment, she made a vow to dedicate her child to God's service if He granted her request. God heard her prayer, and Samuel was born. Hannah's story illustrates that when we commit our deepest desires to God, He responds in ways that exceed our expectations.

Practical Steps:

1. Write Down Your Weight Loss Goals:

Writing down your goals is a powerful step in committing them to God. Be specific about what you want to achieve. This act of writing serves as a tangible commitment and helps you stay focused.

Reflection:

- What are your specific weight loss goals?

- How do these goals align with honoring God with your body?

Example Goals:

- "I want to lose 15 pounds in the next three months."

- "I aim to exercise for at least 30 minutes every day."

- "I will replace sugary snacks with fruits and vegetables."

2. Pray for God's Guidance and Strength:

Prayer is essential in committing your journey to God. Through prayer, you invite God into every aspect of your weight loss journey, seeking His guidance, strength, and wisdom.

Suggested Prayer:

"Dear Lord, I commit my weight loss journey to You. Please guide me, give me strength, and help me make healthy choices. I trust that with Your help, I can achieve my goals. Thank You for walking with me every step of the way. In Jesus' name, Amen."

Reflection:

- In what areas do you need God's guidance and strength?

- How can you make prayer a regular part of your daily routine?

3. Plan Your Meals and Workouts for the Week:

Planning is a practical expression of commitment. When you take time to plan your meals and workouts, you set yourself up for success. This step helps prevent impulsive decisions that can derail your progress.

Meal and Workout Plan Example:

- Monday:

- Breakfast: Oatmeal with fresh berries

- Lunch: Grilled chicken salad

- Dinner: Baked salmon with steamed vegetables

- Workout: 30-minute brisk walk

- Tuesday:

- Breakfast: Greek yogurt with honey and nuts

- Lunch: Turkey and avocado wrap

- Dinner: Stir-fried tofu with mixed vegetables

- Workout: 30 minutes of yoga

Reflection:

- How can planning help you stay committed to your goals?

- What specific steps will you take to plan your meals and workouts this week?

Expository Bible Study:

To deepen your understanding of commitment, let's explore additional Bible passages that emphasize this theme.

1. Psalm 37:5:

_"Commit your way to the LORD; trust in him and he will do this."_

Explanation:

This verse echoes the sentiment of Proverbs 16:3, emphasizing the importance of committing our ways to the Lord. Trusting in God means believing that He will act on our behalf. The psalmist encourages us to rely fully on God's faithfulness.

Application:

- Reflect on how trusting God can transform your weight loss journey.

- Write a prayer committing your specific goals and plans to the Lord.

2. James 4:15:

_"Instead, you ought to say, 'If it is the Lord's will, we will live and do this or that.'"_

Explanation:

James reminds us to acknowledge God's sovereignty in our plans. By saying, "If it is the Lord's will," we recognize that our lives are ultimately in God's hands. This humble acknowledgment aligns our desires with God's purposes.

Application:

- Consider how you can align your weight loss goals with God's will.

- Pray for discernment to understand God's will for your health and well-being.

3. Philippians 4:13:

_"I can do all this through him who gives me strength."_

Explanation:

Paul speaks of the strength that comes from Christ. This verse assures us that we can achieve our goals through Christ's empowerment. It's a reminder that we are not alone in our struggles; God's strength is available to us.

Application:

- Meditate on Philippians 4:13 and how it applies to your weight loss journey.

- Write down instances where you have experienced God's strength in the past.

Reflection Questions:

1. What are your weight loss goals, and how can you commit them to God?

2. How does committing your plans to the Lord change your perspective on your weight loss journey?

3. In what areas do you need God's strength and guidance the most?

Daily Affirmation:

"I am committed to my health and well-being. With God's help, I can achieve my weight loss goals. I trust Him to guide me and give me strength."

Encouragement:

Remember, commitment is about staying dedicated even when things get tough. There will be days when you feel like giving up, but those are the moments when you need to lean on God the most. Keep pressing forward, knowing that with each step, you are not only moving closer to your weight loss goals but also deepening your relationship with God.

As you go through this first day, remember that you are setting the foundation for the next 29 days. Stay focused, stay committed, and trust in God's plan for your journey. You have already taken the first step by opening this book and starting this journey. Keep going, and let God establish your plans.

Conclusion

Commitment is Key

The journey of a thousand miles begins with a single step, and today you have taken that step by committing your weight loss journey to God. Keep this commitment in the forefront of your mind as you continue through each day of this study. Remember, you are not alone. God is with you, guiding and supporting you every step of the way.

Embrace this journey with faith and determination, knowing that your commitment to God and to yourself will yield incredible results. As you progress, you will not only see changes in your physical health but also experience spiritual growth and a deeper connection with God.

Stay committed, stay focused, and trust in the Lord to establish your plans.

# DAY 02

---

## SELF-CONTROL

Bible Verse:

_"For the Spirit God gave us does not make us timid, but gives us power, love, and self-discipline."_ – 2 Timothy 1:7

Devotional:

Self-control is one of the most crucial aspects of any weight loss journey. The Apostle Paul, in his letter to Timothy, reminds us that God has not given us a spirit of timidity but one of power, love, and self-discipline. Self-discipline, or self-control, is a fruit of the Spirit (Galatians 5:22-23) and is essential for making healthy choices consistently.

When we talk about self-control, we are referring to the ability to regulate our emotions, thoughts, and behaviors in the face of temptations and impulses. It's about making decisions that align with our goals and values, even when it's difficult. The Holy Spirit empowers us to exercise self-control, enabling us to overcome the desires of the flesh and live according to God's will.

Consider Jesus' example in the wilderness (Matthew 4:1-11). After fasting for forty days and nights, He was hungry and tempted by Satan. Despite His physical weakness, Jesus exercised remarkable self-control by relying on Scripture and the power of the Holy Spirit. He resisted temptation and remained obedient to God's word.

Practical Steps:

1. Identify Areas Where You Struggle with Self-Control:

The first step in developing self-control is to recognize the areas where you struggle. This might be emotional eating, cravings for unhealthy foods, or lack of motivation to exercise.

Reflection:

- What situations or emotions trigger your lack of self-control?

- How do these struggles impact your weight loss journey?

Example Areas:

- Late-night snacking

- Overeating during social gatherings

- Skipping workouts due to lack of motivation

2. Pray for Strength in Those Areas:

Once you have identified your struggles, bring them before God in prayer. Ask for His strength and guidance to help you overcome these challenges. Remember, self-control is a fruit of the Spirit, and you can rely on God's power to develop it.

Suggested Prayer:

"Heavenly Father, I acknowledge my struggles with self-control, especially when it comes to [specific area]. Please give me the strength and discipline to overcome these challenges. Fill me with Your Holy Spirit and help me make choices that honor You. In Jesus' name, Amen."

Reflection:

- How can prayer help you gain control over your struggles?

- In what ways have you seen God's strength in your life before?

3. Replace Unhealthy Snacks with Nutritious Options:

One practical way to exercise self-control is by making healthier food choices. Instead of reaching for unhealthy snacks, choose nutritious options that fuel your body and align with your goals.

Healthy Snack Ideas:

- Fresh fruit (apples, berries, bananas)

- Vegetables with hummus

- Nuts and seeds (almonds, walnuts, chia seeds)

- Greek yogurt with honey and nuts

Reflection:

- How can you prepare for moments of weakness by having healthy snacks readily available?

- What small changes can you make today to improve your eating habits?

Expository Bible Study:

To deepen your understanding of self-control, let's explore additional Bible passages that emphasize this theme.

1. Galatians 5:22-23:

_"But the fruit of the Spirit is love, joy, peace, forbearance, kindness, goodness, faithfulness, gentleness and self-control. Against such things, there is no law."_

Explanation:

Self-control is listed as one of the fruits of the Spirit. This means that as we grow in our relationship with God, the Holy Spirit cultivates self-control within us. It is not something we develop on our own but through the Spirit's work in our lives.

Application:

- Reflect on how you can allow the Holy Spirit to work in you to develop self-control.

- Pray for an increased manifestation of the fruits of the Spirit in your life.

2. 1 Corinthians 9:25-27:

_"Everyone who competes in the games goes into strict training. They do it to get a crown that will not last, but we do it to get a crown that will last forever. Therefore, I do not run like someone running aimlessly; I do not fight like a boxer beating the air. No, I strike a blow to my body and make it my slave so that after I have preached to others, I myself will not be disqualified for the prize."_

Explanation:

Paul uses the analogy of an athlete to illustrate the importance of self-control. Just as athletes undergo strict training and discipline to achieve a temporary crown, we are called to exercise self-control for an eternal reward. This involves being intentional and purposeful in our actions.

Application:

- Consider how you can adopt the mindset of an athlete in your weight loss journey.

- Set specific, achievable goals and create a plan to reach them.

3. Proverbs 25:28:

_"Like a city whose walls are broken through is a person who lacks self-control."_

Explanation:

This proverb highlights the vulnerability that comes with a lack of self-control. Just as a city without walls is defenseless against its enemies, a person without self-control is susceptible to various temptations and destructive behaviors. Building self-control is like fortifying the walls of a city, providing protection and stability.

Application:

- Identify areas in your life where lack of self-control makes you vulnerable.

- Develop strategies to strengthen your self-control, such as setting boundaries and seeking accountability.

Reflection Questions:

1. In what areas of your life do you struggle with self-control?

2. How can you rely on the Holy Spirit to help you develop self-discipline?

3. What practical steps can you take to replace unhealthy habits with healthy ones?

Daily Affirmation:

"I am empowered by the Holy Spirit to exercise self-control. With God's help, I can make healthy choices that honor Him and support my weight loss goals."

Encouragement:

Self-control is a journey, not a destination. It requires consistent effort and reliance on God's strength. Remember that every small victory in exercising self-control is a step towards achieving your larger goals. Celebrate these victories and be patient with yourself during setbacks. Trust that the Holy Spirit is working within you to develop this essential fruit.

As you continue through this 30-day journey, keep seeking God's guidance and strength. He is faithful to help you overcome your struggles and empower you to make choices that honor Him. Stay committed, stay disciplined, and trust in the Lord's plan for your health and well-being.

Conclusion

Self-control through the Spirit

Developing self-control is crucial for success in your weight loss journey and in all areas of life. By relying on the Holy Spirit, you can cultivate self-discipline and make healthy choices that honor God. As you continue to commit each day to the Lord, remember that He has given you a spirit of

power, love, and self-discipline. Trust in His strength and
guidance to help you achieve your goals.

15

# DAY 03

---

## HEALTHY HABITS

Bible Verse:

_"Do you not know that your bodies are temples of the Holy Spirit, who is in you, whom you have received from God? You are not your own."_ – 1 Corinthians 6:19

Devotional:

Our bodies are described in the Bible as temples of the Holy Spirit. This profound truth reminds us of the sacredness of our physical bodies and our responsibility to care for them. When Paul wrote to the Corinthians, he was addressing a culture that often misused and mistreated the body. His words call us to a higher standard, recognizing that our bodies are not our own but belong to God.

In practical terms, viewing our bodies as temples means adopting healthy habits that honor God. This includes regular exercise, balanced nutrition, adequate rest, and avoiding harmful substances. Healthy habits are not merely about losing weight or looking good but about maintaining the body in which God's Spirit dwells. When we prioritize our health, we demonstrate our gratitude for the gift of life and the presence of the Holy Spirit within us.

Consider Daniel's example in the Old Testament. When offered rich foods and wine from the king's table, Daniel chose to eat vegetables and drink water, honoring God with his dietary choices. His commitment to healthy habits not only preserved his physical health but also honored God and set a positive example for others (Daniel 1:8-16).

Practical Steps:

1. Start a Daily Exercise Routine:

Physical activity is crucial for maintaining a healthy body. Regular exercise improves cardiovascular health, strengthens muscles, and boosts mental well-being.

Reflection:

- What types of exercise do you enjoy?

- How can you incorporate physical activity into your daily routine?

Example Routine:

- Monday: 30-minute brisk walk

- Tuesday: 20 minutes of strength training

- Wednesday: 30 minutes of yoga

- Thursday: 30-minute cycling

- Friday: 20 minutes of HIIT (High-Intensity Interval Training)

- Saturday: a 45-minute hike

- Sunday: Rest day or light stretching

2. Drink Plenty of Water:

Staying hydrated is essential for overall health. Water aids digestion, helps regulate body temperature, and supports metabolic processes.

Reflection:

- How much water do you currently drink daily?

- What strategies can you use to increase your water intake?

Tips for Staying Hydrated:

- Carry a reusable water bottle with you.

- Set reminders to drink water throughout the day.

- Replace sugary drinks with water.

3. Avoid Processed Foods:

Processed foods often contain unhealthy fats, sugars, and additives that can harm your body. Opt for whole, nutrient-dense foods that provide essential vitamins and minerals.

Reflection:

- What processed foods do you frequently consume?

- How can you transition to a diet rich in whole foods?

Healthy Eating Tips:

- Fill your plate with fruits and vegetables.

- Choose whole grains over refined grains.

- Include lean proteins such as chicken, fish, and legumes.

Expository Bible Study:

To deepen your understanding of healthy habits, let's explore additional Bible passages that emphasize this theme.

1. Romans 12:1:

_"Therefore, I urge you, brothers and sisters, in view of God's mercy, to offer your bodies as a living sacrifice, holy and pleasing to God—this is your true and proper worship."_

Explanation:

Paul urges believers to offer their bodies as living sacrifices. This means living in a way that honors God, including how we care for our physical health. It is an act of worship to maintain our bodies in a manner that pleases God.

Application:

- Reflect on how maintaining healthy habits can be an act of worship.

- Consider ways to offer your body as a living sacrifice through healthy living.

2. Proverbs 3:7-8:

_"Do not be wise in your own eyes; fear the LORD and shun evil. This will bring health to your body and nourishment to your bones."_

Explanation:

This proverb highlights the connection between spiritual and physical health. Fearing the Lord and shunning evil contribute to our well-being. Healthy living involves more than just physical actions; it includes spiritual and moral choices that honor God.

Application:

- Evaluate how your spiritual life influences your physical health.

- Pray for wisdom to make choices that bring health to your body and soul.

3. 1 Timothy 4:8:

_"For physical training is of some value, but godliness has value for all things, holding promise for both the present life and the life to come."_

Explanation:

Paul acknowledges the value of physical training but emphasizes that godliness holds greater value. While maintaining physical health is important, nurturing our spiritual health has eternal significance.

Application:

- Balance your focus on physical and spiritual health.

- Commit to daily practices that nurture both your body and soul.

Reflection Questions:

1. How does viewing your body as a temple of the Holy Spirit change your perspective on healthy living?

2. What steps can you take today to start a daily exercise routine?

3. How can you incorporate more whole foods into your diet and reduce your consumption of processed foods?

Daily Affirmation:

"My body is a temple of the Holy Spirit. I honor God by adopting healthy habits and caring for the gift of life He has given me."

Encouragement:

Healthy habits are built over time through consistent, small choices. Don't be discouraged by setbacks or slow progress. Each healthy choice you make is a step towards honoring God with your body and improving your overall well-being. Remember that your journey towards better health is also a spiritual journey, reflecting your commitment to God.

As you continue this 30-day journey, keep seeking God's guidance and strength. He is faithful to help you cultivate healthy habits that honor Him. Stay committed, stay focused, and trust in the Lord's plan for your health and well-being.

Conclusion

Healthy Habits for a Healthy Temple

Developing healthy habits is essential for honoring God with our bodies. By viewing our bodies as temples of the Holy Spirit, we recognize the importance of caring for them through exercise, hydration, and nutritious eating. As you continue to commit each day to the Lord, trust that He will guide and support you in cultivating habits that reflect His love and care.

CHAPTER 04

___

## RENEWING YOUR MIND

Bible Verse:

_"Do not conform to the pattern of this world, but be transformed by the renewing of your mind. Then you will be able to test and approve what God's will is—his good, pleasing, and perfect will."_ – Romans 12:2

Devotional:

The mind is a powerful battleground in the journey toward better health. Paul's instruction to the Romans to not conform to the pattern of this world but to be transformed by the renewing of their minds is pivotal for lasting change. In the context of a weight loss journey, this transformation begins with changing the way we think about food, exercise, and our bodies.

Renewing your mind involves replacing negative, destructive thoughts with positive, God-honoring ones. It's about rejecting the world's standards and embracing God's truth. This mental shift is crucial for breaking free from unhealthy habits and establishing new, healthy ones. It means viewing your body as a temple of the Holy Spirit and recognizing the importance of caring for it.

Consider the story of Elijah in 1 Kings 19. After his victory over the prophets of Baal, Elijah experienced fear and depression, feeling overwhelmed and wanting to give up. God addressed Elijah's mental state by providing physical rest and nourishment and then speaking to him in a gentle whisper, renewing his mind and spirit. Similarly, God wants to renew your mind, giving you the strength and clarity to continue your journey.

Practical Steps:

1. Meditate on Today's Verse:

Take time to meditate on Romans 12:2. Reflect on what it means to not conform to the patterns of this world but to be transformed by the renewing of your mind.

Reflection:

- How have worldly patterns influenced your thoughts about health and weight loss?

- What does it mean to you to be transformed by the renewing of your mind?

2. Write Down Negative Thoughts and Replace Them with Positive Affirmations:

Identify the negative thoughts that often sabotage your efforts. Write them down and then counter them with positive, Scripture-based affirmations.

Examples:

- Negative Thought: "I can't stick to a healthy diet."

- Positive Affirmation: "I can do all this through Him who gives me strength." – Philippians 4:13

- Negative Thought: "I'm never going to lose this weight."

- Positive Affirmation: "With God, all things are possible." – Matthew 19:26

Reflection:

- What negative thoughts frequently undermine your efforts?

- How can you replace them with affirmations rooted in God's Word?

3. Spend Time in Prayer and Reflection:

Dedicate time each day to pray and reflect. Ask God to renew your mind and help you see yourself and your journey through His eyes.

Suggested Prayer:

"Lord, transform my mind and help me see myself as You see me. Renew my thoughts and give me the strength to break free from unhealthy patterns. Help me to focus on Your truth and promises. In Jesus' name, Amen."

Reflection:

- How can daily prayer and reflection support the renewal of your mind?

- In what ways have you experienced God's transformative power in your life before?

Expository Bible Study:

To deepen your understanding of renewing your mind, let's explore additional Bible passages that emphasize this theme.

1. Philippians 4:8:

_"Finally, brothers and sisters, whatever is true, whatever is noble, whatever is right, whatever is pure, whatever is lovely, whatever is admirable—if anything is excellent or praiseworthy—think about such things."_

Explanation:

Paul encourages believers to focus their thoughts on positive and virtuous things. By doing so, we cultivate a mindset that aligns with God's will and fosters spiritual growth.

Application:

- Reflect on how focusing on positive thoughts can impact your health journey.

- Make a list of true, noble, and praiseworthy things to meditate on daily.

2. Colossians 3:2:

_"Set your minds on things above, not on earthly things."_

Explanation:

This verse encourages us to focus our minds on heavenly, eternal matters rather than getting bogged down by worldly concerns. This shift in perspective helps us align our priorities with God's will.

Application:

- Consider how setting your mind on things above can transform your approach to health and wellness.

- Pray for a heavenly perspective on your goals and challenges.

3. Ephesians 4:22-24:

_"You were taught, with regard to your former way of life, to put off your old self, which is being corrupted by its deceitful desires; to be made new in the attitude of your minds; and to put on the new self, created to be like God in true righteousness and holiness."_

Explanation:

Paul speaks about shedding the old self and being renewed in the attitude of our minds. This involves a deliberate effort to adopt a new mindset and live according to God's standards.

Application:

- Reflect on areas where you need to put off the old self and embrace a new, godly mindset.

- Commit to daily renewal of your mind through prayer and Scripture.

Reflection Questions:

1. How can you renew your mind to support your weight loss journey?

2. What negative thoughts do you need to replace with positive, Scripture-based affirmations?

3. How can focusing on God's truth transform your approach to health and wellness?

Daily Affirmation:

"I am being transformed by the renewing of my mind. With God's help, I reject negative thoughts and embrace His truth, knowing that I can achieve my health goals through His strength."

Encouragement:

Renewing your mind is an ongoing process that requires patience and persistence. Each day, make a conscious effort to align your thoughts with God's truth. When negative thoughts arise, counter them with positive affirmations based on Scripture. Remember that God's Word is a powerful tool for transformation. As you renew your mind, you will find it easier to make choices that honor God and support your health journey.

As you continue this 30-day journey, keep seeking God's guidance and strength. He is faithful to help you cultivate a mindset that aligns with His will. Stay committed, stay focused, and trust in the Lord's plan for your health and well-being.

Conclusion

Transforming Your Mind

Renewing your mind is crucial for lasting change in your health journey. By focusing on God's truth and rejecting worldly patterns, you can develop a mindset that supports healthy habits and honors God. As you continue to commit each day to the Lord, trust that He will guide and support you in this transformation.

# DAY 05

---

## PATIENCE AND PERSEVERANCE

Bible Verse:

_"Let us not become weary in doing good, for at the proper time we will reap a harvest if we do not give up."_ – Galatians 6:9

Devotional:

Patience and perseverance are essential virtues in any weight loss journey. The Apostle Paul, in his letter to the Galatians, encourages believers not to grow weary in doing good, promising that at the proper time, we will reap a harvest if we do not give up. This verse reminds us that progress often requires sustained effort over time and that perseverance is key to seeing the fruits of our labor.

In the context of weight loss, patience means understanding that lasting change does not happen overnight. It involves making consistent, healthy choices even when results are not immediate. Perseverance, on the other hand, is the determination to keep going despite challenges, setbacks, and discouragement.

Consider the story of the Israelites in the wilderness. After being freed from slavery in Egypt, they wandered for forty years before reaching the Promised Land. Throughout their journey, they faced numerous challenges and temptations to give up, but those who remained faithful eventually saw the fulfillment of God's promise. Similarly, your journey to better health may be long and fraught with obstacles, but perseverance and faith in God's promises will lead you to your goal.

Practical Steps:

1. Set Small, Achievable Goals:

Breaking down your larger weight loss goals into smaller, manageable steps can help maintain motivation and provide a sense of accomplishment along the way.

Reflection:

- What are some small, achievable goals you can set for yourself?

- How can these smaller goals help you stay focused and motivated?

Example Goals:

- "I will drink eight glasses of water every day this week."

- "I will walk for 20 minutes every day for the next two weeks."

2. Celebrate Your Progress, No Matter How Small:

Recognizing and celebrating your achievements, no matter how minor they may seem, can boost your motivation and reinforce positive behavior.

Reflection:

- How do you currently acknowledge your progress?

- What are some ways you can celebrate your achievements?

Celebration Ideas:

- Treat yourself to a new workout outfit.

- Share your progress with a supportive friend or family member.

- Take a moment to thank God for your progress in prayer.

3. Encourage Yourself with Positive Affirmations:

Use positive affirmations to reinforce your commitment and remind yourself of the progress you've made and the goals you're working towards.

Reflection:

- What affirmations can you use to encourage yourself?

- How can you incorporate these affirmations into your daily routine?

Example Affirmations:

- "I am making progress every day, and I am proud of my efforts."

- "I trust that God is with me on this journey and that He will help me achieve my goals."

Expository Bible Study:

To deepen your understanding of patience and perseverance, let's explore additional Bible passages that emphasize this theme.

1. James 1:2-4:

_"Consider it pure joy, my brothers and sisters, whenever you face trials of many kinds, because you know that the testing of your faith produces perseverance. Let perseverance finish its work so that you may be mature and complete, not lacking anything."_

Explanation:

James encourages believers to view trials as opportunities for growth. The testing of our faith produces perseverance, leading to maturity and completeness. This perspective helps us embrace challenges as part of our journey toward becoming more Christ-like.

Application:

- Reflect on how challenges in your weight loss journey can help you grow.

- Pray for a perspective that sees trials as opportunities for growth.

2. Hebrews 12:1-2:

_"Therefore, since we are surrounded by such a great cloud of witnesses, let us throw off everything that hinders and the sin that so easily entangles. And let us run with perseverance the race marked out for us, fixing our eyes on Jesus, the pioneer and perfecter of faith. For the joy set before him, he endured the cross, scorning its shame, and sat down at the right hand of the throne of God."_

Explanation:

The writer of Hebrews likens the Christian life to a race that requires perseverance. By fixing our eyes on Jesus, who endured the cross for the joy set before Him, we find the strength to continue running our race, shedding anything that hinders us.

Application:

- Identify what hinders your progress in your weight loss journey.

- Commit to focusing on Jesus as your source of strength and perseverance.

3. Isaiah 40:31:

_"But those who hope in the LORD will renew their strength. They will soar on wings like eagles; they will run and not grow weary, they will walk and not be faint."_

Explanation:

Isaiah offers a promise of renewed strength for those who hope in the Lord. By placing our trust in God, we find the endurance to keep going without growing weary.

Application:

- Reflect on how hope in the Lord can renew your strength.

- Pray for God's strength to sustain you in your journey.

Reflection Questions:

1. How can setting small, achievable goals help you stay patient and motivated?

2. What are some ways you can celebrate your progress and stay encouraged?

3. How can you remind yourself to rely on God's strength and promises during your weight loss journey?

Daily Affirmation:

"I am patient and persistent in my weight loss journey. With God's help, I can overcome challenges and achieve my goals."

Encouragement:

Patience and perseverance are essential for achieving lasting change. Remember that progress often comes gradually, and setbacks are a natural part of the journey. Keep your eyes fixed on your goals and trust that God is with you every step of the way. Celebrate your progress, stay motivated, and rely on God's strength to sustain you.

As you continue this 30-day journey, keep seeking God's guidance and strength. He is faithful to help you cultivate patience and perseverance. Stay committed, stay focused, and trust in the Lord's plan for your health and well-being.

Conclusion

Patience and Perseverance for Lasting Change

Developing patience and perseverance is crucial for success in your weight loss journey. By setting small, achievable goals and celebrating your progress, you can stay motivated and focused. As you continue to commit each day to the Lord, trust that He will guide and support you in cultivating these essential virtues.

# DAY 06

---

## GRATITUDE

Bible Verse:

_"Give thanks in all circumstances; for this is God's will for you in Christ Jesus."_ – 1 Thessalonians 5:18

Devotional:

Gratitude is a powerful attitude that can transform your perspective and fuel your weight loss journey. Paul's exhortation to the Thessalonians to give thanks in all circumstances highlights the importance of maintaining a grateful heart regardless of our situation. Gratitude shifts our focus from what we lack to what we have, fostering contentment and joy.

In the context of weight loss, gratitude helps you appreciate the progress you've made, no matter how small. It encourages you to celebrate your body for what it can do rather than criticize it for what it cannot. This positive outlook can increase your motivation and resilience, helping you stay committed to your goals.

Consider the story of the ten lepers in Luke 17:11-19. All ten were healed by Jesus, but only one returned to give thanks. This grateful leper received an additional blessing—Jesus said to him, "Rise and go; your faith has made you well." Gratitude not only acknowledges what God has done but also opens the door for further blessings.

Practical Steps:

1. Start a Gratitude Journal:

Keeping a gratitude journal is a practical way to cultivate a thankful heart. Each day, write down at least three things you are grateful for. This practice helps you focus on the positive aspects of your journey and life in general.

Reflection:

- What are three things you are grateful for today?

- How can maintaining a gratitude journal enhance your weight loss journey?

Example Entries:

- "I am grateful for the strength to exercise today."

- "I am thankful for the support of my friends and family."

- "I appreciate the healthy meals I can prepare and enjoy."

2. Thank God for Your Body and Health:

Take time to thank God for your body and the health you have. Recognize that your body is a gift from God, and expressing gratitude for it can help you develop a positive relationship with it.

Reflection:

- What are some aspects of your body and health that you are grateful for?

- How can expressing gratitude for your body help you honor it with healthy choices?

Suggested Prayer:

"Heavenly Father, thank You for the gift of my body and the health You have given me. Help me to appreciate and care for it as You desire. Thank You for the strength and ability to pursue a healthier lifestyle. In Jesus' name, Amen."

3. List Three Things You're Grateful for Each Day:

Incorporate gratitude into your daily routine by listing three things you are thankful for each day. This habit will help you maintain a positive outlook and stay motivated on your weight loss journey.

Reflection:

- How can daily gratitude practices impact your overall well-being?

- What small moments or blessings can you acknowledge today?

Expository Bible Study:

To deepen your understanding of gratitude, let's explore additional Bible passages that emphasize this theme.

1. Philippians 4:6-7:

_"Do not be anxious about anything, but in every situation, by prayer and petition, with thanksgiving, present your requests to God. And the peace of God, which transcends all understanding, will guard your hearts and your minds in Christ Jesus."_

Explanation:

Paul instructs believers to approach God with thanksgiving in every situation. This attitude of gratitude, combined with prayer, brings peace that guards our hearts and minds.

Application:

- Reflect on how Thanksgiving can alleviate anxiety and bring peace.

- Practice incorporating gratitude into your prayers and petitions.

2. Colossians 3:15-17:

_"Let the peace of Christ rule in your hearts, since as members of one body you were called to peace. And be thankful. Let the message of Christ dwell among you richly as you teach and admonish one another with all wisdom through psalms, hymns, and songs from the Spirit, singing to God with gratitude in your hearts. And whatever you do, whether in word or deed, do it all in the name of the Lord Jesus, giving thanks to God the Father through him."_

Explanation:

Paul emphasizes the importance of gratitude in the life of a believer. He encourages the Colossians to let Christ's peace rule in their hearts and to be thankful in all circumstances.

Application:

- Consider how gratitude can enhance your sense of peace and unity with others.

- Make a conscious effort to thank God in all your activities.

3. Psalm 100:4:

_"Enter his gates with thanksgiving and his courts with praise; give thanks to him and praise his name."_

Explanation:

This psalm highlights the importance of entering God's presence with a thankful heart. Thanksgiving and praise are integral to worship and draw us closer to God.

Application:

- Reflect on how gratitude can deepen your relationship with God.

- Make thanksgiving and praise a regular part of your worship.

Reflection Questions:

1. How can maintaining a gratitude journal help you stay positive and motivated on your weight loss journey?

2. What aspects of your body and health are you thankful for?

3. How can incorporating gratitude into your daily routine impact your overall well-being?

Daily Affirmation:

"I am grateful for the progress I have made and the strength God gives me each day. I choose to focus on the positive and thank God for His blessings."

Encouragement:

Gratitude is a powerful tool that can transform your perspective and fuel your motivation. By focusing on the positive aspects of your journey and thanking God for His blessings, you can cultivate a joyful and resilient spirit. Remember that every small step forward is a reason to be thankful, and God delights in your gratitude.

As you continue this 30-day journey, keep seeking God's guidance and strength. He is faithful to help you

cultivate a grateful heart and stay committed to your goals. Stay focused, stay positive, and trust in the Lord's plan for your health and well-being.

Conclusion

Gratitude for a Joyful Journey

Cultivating gratitude is essential for maintaining a positive outlook and staying motivated on your weight loss journey. By focusing on the blessings in your life and expressing thanks to God, you can develop a joyful and resilient spirit. As you continue to commit each day to the Lord, trust that He will guide and support you in cultivating a thankful heart.

## REST

Bible Verse:

_"Come to me, all you who are weary and burdened, and I will give you rest."_ – Matthew 11:28

Devotional:

Rest is an essential, yet often overlooked, component of a healthy lifestyle. Jesus' invitation in Matthew 11:28 is a reminder of the importance of rest for our physical, mental, and spiritual well-being. In a world that often glorifies busyness, taking time to rest can be seen as a weakness, but the Bible teaches us that rest is a vital part of God's design for our lives.

Rest is not merely the absence of activity; it is an intentional time to rejuvenate and renew our strength. It allows our bodies to recover, our minds to refocus, and our spirits to reconnect with God. When we neglect rest, we risk burnout, reduced effectiveness, and weakened resolve in our health journey.

Consider the creation narrative in Genesis 2:2-3, where God Himself rested on the seventh day after creating the heavens and the earth. This act established a pattern for us to follow—a rhythm of work and rest. Jesus, too, often withdrew to solitary places to rest and pray (Luke 5:16). By following these examples, we acknowledge our need for rest and trust in God's provision.

Practical Steps:

1. Ensure You Get 7-8 Hours of Sleep Each Night:

Adequate sleep is crucial for overall health. It supports physical recovery, mental clarity, and emotional stability.

Reflection:

- How many hours of sleep do you currently get each night?

- What changes can you make to ensure you get enough sleep?

Tips for Better Sleep:

- Establish a consistent bedtime routine.

- Create a restful environment by keeping your bedroom dark, quiet, and cool.

- Limit screen time before bed.

2. Take a Day Off from Intense Exercise:

Rest days are important for muscle recovery and preventing injury. Use this time to engage in gentle activities or simply relax.

Reflection:

- How often do you incorporate rest days into your exercise routine?

- What activities can you do on rest days to promote relaxation?

Example Activities:

- Light stretching or yoga

- Gentle walking

- Reading or listening to music

3. Spend Time in Quiet Prayer and Meditation:

Use rest as an opportunity to connect with God through prayer and meditation. This practice can rejuvenate your spirit and provide clarity and peace.

Reflection:

- How can prayer and meditation enhance your sense of rest?

- What specific times can you set aside for quiet reflection and prayer?

Suggested Prayer:

"Lord, thank You for the gift of rest. Help me to embrace it as an essential part of my health journey. Renew my strength and spirit as I spend time in Your presence. In Jesus' name, Amen."

Expository Bible Study:

To deepen your understanding of rest, let's explore additional Bible passages that emphasize this theme.

1. Psalm 23:1-3:

_"The LORD is my shepherd, I lack nothing. He makes me lie down in green pastures, he leads me beside quiet waters, he refreshes my soul. He guides me along the right paths for his name's sake."_

Explanation:

David describes God as a shepherd who provides rest and refreshment. This imagery emphasizes God's care and provision, leading us to places of peace and renewal.

Application:

- Reflect on how God leads you to places of rest and refreshment.

- Spend time in nature or other peaceful settings to experience God's renewal.

2. Exodus 33:14:

_"The LORD replied, 'My Presence will go with you, and I will give you rest.'"_

Explanation:

God promises Moses that His presence will go with him and provide rest. This assurance reminds us that true rest is found in God's presence.

Application:

- Consider how you can invite God's presence into your daily life.

- Practice being still and aware of God's presence to experience His rest.

3. Hebrews 4:9-10:

_"There remains, then, a Sabbath rest for the people of God; for anyone who enters God's rest also rests from their works, just as God did from his."_

Explanation:

The writer of Hebrews speaks of a Sabbath rest that remains for God's people. This rest is both a present reality and a future hope, emphasizing the importance of ceasing from our own works and trusting in God.

Application:

- Reflect on the concept of Sabbath rest and how you can incorporate it into your weekly routine.

- Trust in God's provision and let go of the need to constantly strive.

Reflection Questions:

1. How can you prioritize rest in your daily and weekly routine?

2. What steps can you take to ensure you get adequate sleep each night?

3. How can spending time in quiet prayer and meditation enhance your sense of rest and renewal?

Daily Affirmation:

"I embrace rest as an essential part of my health journey. With God's help, I prioritize rest to renew my strength and spirit."

Encouragement:

Rest is not a sign of weakness but a vital component of a healthy and balanced life. Embrace rest as a gift from God, designed to renew your strength and refresh your spirit. By prioritizing rest, you honor the rhythm that God established and allow yourself to be rejuvenated for the journey ahead.

As you continue this 30-day journey, keep seeking God's guidance and strength. He is faithful to help you cultivate healthy rest habits that honor Him. Stay committed, stay rested, and trust in the Lord's plan for your health and well-being.

Conclusion

Rest for Renewal

Embracing rest is crucial for maintaining balance and well-being in your weight loss journey. By prioritizing rest and trusting in God's provision, you can renew your strength and spirit. As you continue to commit each day to the Lord, trust that He will guide and support you in cultivating healthy rest habits.

# DAY 08

---

## FAITH AND TRUST

Bible Verse:

_"Trust in the LORD with all your heart and lean not on your own understanding; in all your ways submit to him, and he will make your paths straight."_ – Proverbs 3:5-6

Devotional:

Faith and trust are foundational to any journey, especially one that involves significant change like weight loss. Proverbs 3:5-6 encourages us to trust in the Lord with all our hearts and not rely on our own understanding. This verse is a call to submit every aspect of our lives to God, trusting that He will guide us and make our paths straight.

Trusting God with your weight loss journey means believing that He cares about your health and well-being. It means surrendering your doubts, fears, and anxieties to Him, and relying on His wisdom rather than your own. Faith is the assurance of things hoped for, the conviction of things not seen (Hebrews 11:1). It is trusting in God's promises and His faithfulness.

Consider Abraham's example. God called him to leave his homeland and go to a place He would show him. Abraham trusted God, despite not knowing where he was going or how things would unfold. His faith was credited to him as righteousness (Genesis 12:1-4, Hebrews 11:8). Similarly, your faith in God can guide you through your weight loss journey, even when the path ahead is unclear.

Practical Steps:

1. Pray for Guidance and Clarity:

Begin each day with prayer, asking God to guide your steps and give you clarity in your decisions. Trust that He will provide the wisdom you need.

Reflection:

- How can you incorporate prayer into your daily routine?

- What specific areas of your weight loss journey do you need God's guidance and clarity?

Suggested Prayer:

"Dear Lord, I trust You with my weight loss journey. Please guide me, give me clarity, and help me to make choices that honor You. I surrender my fears and doubts to You, knowing that You are faithful. In Jesus' name, Amen."

2. Let Go of Stress and Worry About Your Progress:

Worrying about your progress can lead to anxiety and discouragement. Trust that God is at work, even when you can't see immediate results.

Reflection:

- What specific worries or stresses do you have about your weight loss journey?

- How can you let go of these worries and trust God more fully?

Tips for Reducing Stress:

- Practice deep breathing exercises.

- Spend time in nature.

- Engage in activities that bring you joy and relaxation.

3. Follow Your Plan with Faith:

Stick to your weight loss plan, believing that God is with you and will help you succeed. Faith is not passive; it involves taking action based on trust in God.

Reflection:

- How can you demonstrate your faith through your actions today?

- What steps can you take to follow your plan with confidence and trust in God?

Example Actions:

- Prepare healthy meals ahead of time.

- Schedule your workouts and stick to them.

- Track your progress and celebrate small victories.

Expository Bible Study:

To deepen your understanding of faith and trust, let's explore additional Bible passages that emphasize this theme.

1. Jeremiah 17:7-8:

_"But blessed is the one who trusts in the LORD, whose confidence is in him. They will be like a tree planted by the water that sends out its roots by the stream. It does not fear when heat comes; its leaves are always green. It has no worries in a year of drought and never fails to bear fruit."_

Explanation:

Jeremiah compares those who trust in the Lord to a tree planted by the water. This imagery conveys stability, nourishment, and fruitfulness, even in difficult circumstances.

Application:

- Reflect on how trust in God can provide stability and nourishment in your life.

- Consider how you can deepen your roots in God's Word and His promises.

2. Psalm 37:5:

_"Commit your way to the LORD; trust in him and he will do this."_

Explanation:

The psalmist encourages us to commit our way to the Lord and trust in Him, promising that He will act on our behalf. This commitment involves surrendering our plans and trusting in God's faithfulness.

Application:

- Reflect on what it means to commit your weight loss journey to the Lord.

- Identify specific areas where you need to trust God more fully.

3. Isaiah 26:3:

_"You will keep in perfect peace those whose minds are steadfast because they trust in you."_

Explanation:

Isaiah highlights the peace that comes from trusting in God. A steadfast mind focused on God's promises experiences perfect peace, even amid challenges.

Application:

- Reflect on how trust in God can bring peace to your heart and mind.

- Practice focusing your thoughts on God's faithfulness and promises.

Reflection Questions:

1. How can you demonstrate your trust in God in your weight loss journey?

2. What specific fears or doubts do you need to surrender to God?

3. How can focusing on God's faithfulness help you stay motivated and confident?

Daily Affirmation:

"I trust in the Lord with all my heart. I surrender my fears and doubts to Him, knowing that He will guide my steps and provide for my needs."

Encouragement:

Faith and trust in God are essential for navigating the challenges of a weight loss journey. By surrendering your fears and doubts to Him and believing in His faithfulness, you can find the strength and confidence to persevere. Remember that God is with you every step of the way, guiding and supporting you.

As you continue this 30-day journey, keep seeking God's guidance and strength. He is faithful to help you cultivate trust and faith, enabling you to achieve your goals.

Stay committed, stay faithful, and trust in the Lord's plan for your health and well-being.

Conclusion

Faith and Trust for the Journey

Developing faith and trust in God is crucial for success in your weight loss journey. By surrendering your doubts and fears to Him and relying on His guidance, you can navigate challenges with confidence and peace. As you continue to commit each day to the Lord, trust that He will guide and support you in cultivating these essential virtues.

DAY 09

## POSITIVE RELATIONSHIP

Bible Verse:

_"As iron sharpens iron, so one person sharpens another."_ – Proverbs 27:17

Devotional:

Relationships play a crucial role in our lives, particularly in challenging journeys like weight loss. Proverbs 27:17 emphasizes the importance of mutual support and encouragement, comparing it to iron sharpening iron. This verse highlights the significance of positive relationships in helping us grow and stay motivated.

Positive relationships provide accountability, encouragement, and inspiration. Surrounding yourself with supportive people can make a significant difference in your weight loss journey. They can offer practical advice, celebrate your successes, and help you stay focused on your goals. In turn, you can also be a source of encouragement and support for others.

Consider the relationship between Jonathan and David in the Bible. Despite the dangers and challenges they faced, Jonathan's support and encouragement were crucial for David. Jonathan's friendship provided David with strength and confidence to persevere (1 Samuel 18:1-4, 1 Samuel 23:16-18). Similarly, the right relationships in your life can provide the strength and encouragement you need to succeed.

Practical Steps:

1. Find an Accountability Partner:

An accountability partner can provide the support and motivation you need to stay on track. Choose someone who shares your commitment to health and can encourage you along the way.

Reflection:

- Who in your life can be a reliable accountability partner?

- How can you support each other in your health journeys?

Example Actions:

- Schedule regular check-ins with your accountability partner.

- Share your goals and progress with each other.

- Encourage and motivate each other during difficult times.

2. Join a Supportive Community or Group:

Being part of a community or group with similar goals can provide a sense of belonging and additional support. Look for local or online groups focused on health and wellness.

Reflection:

- What communities or groups are available to you?

- How can joining a supportive group enhance your weight loss journey?

Example Actions:

- Participate in group workouts or fitness classes.

- Join online forums or social media groups focused on health.

- Attend community events related to wellness and fitness.

3. Share Your Goals and Progress with Trusted Friends or Family:

Sharing your goals and progress with trusted friends or family members can help you stay accountable and receive encouragement. Their support can boost your motivation and confidence.

Reflection:

- Who are the trusted friends or family members you can share your journey with?

- How can their support make a difference in your weight loss efforts?

Suggested Prayer:

"Lord, thank You for the people You have placed in my life. Help me to build positive relationships that support and encourage me in my journey. Give me the wisdom to be a source of encouragement to others as well. In Jesus' name, Amen."

Expository Bible Study:

To deepen your understanding of positive relationships, let's explore additional Bible passages that emphasize this theme.

1. Ecclesiastes 4:9-10:

_"Two are better than one, because they have a good return for their labor: If either of them falls down, one can help the other up. But pity anyone who falls and has no one to help them up."_

Explanation:

This passage highlights the benefits of companionship and mutual support. Having someone to help you when you fall can make a significant difference in your journey.

Application:

- Reflect on the importance of having supportive relationships in your life.

- Identify ways you can be a source of support for others.

2. Hebrews 10:24-25:

_"And let us consider how we may spur one another on toward love and good deeds, not giving up meeting together, as some are in the habit of doing, but encouraging one another—and all the more as you see the Day approaching."_

Explanation:

The writer of Hebrews encourages believers to meet together and encourage one another. This mutual encouragement is vital for maintaining faith and motivation.

Application:

- Reflect on how regular fellowship with others can enhance your journey.

- Consider ways you can actively encourage others in their pursuits.

3. Galatians 6:2:

_"Carry each other's burdens, and in this way you will fulfill the law of Christ."_

Explanation:

Paul emphasizes the importance of bearing one another's burdens. This act of support and empathy fulfills the law of Christ, demonstrating love and compassion.

Application:

- Reflect on how you can help carry the burdens of those around you.

- Identify specific ways you can support others in their health journeys.

Reflection Questions:

1. How can positive relationships support your weight loss journey?

2. Who are the people in your life that you can rely on for encouragement and accountability?

3. How can you be a source of support and encouragement for others?

Daily Affirmation:

"I am surrounded by supportive and encouraging relationships. Together, we strengthen and motivate each other to achieve our goals."

Encouragement:

Positive relationships are invaluable in your weight loss journey. Surrounding yourself with supportive and encouraging people can provide the motivation and accountability you need to stay on track. Remember that you are not alone in this journey; others can offer the support and encouragement you need.

As you continue this 30-day journey, keep seeking God's guidance and strength. He is faithful to help you build and maintain positive relationships that support your health and well-being. Stay committed, stay connected, and trust in the Lord's plan for your relationships and journey.

Conclusion

Strength in Positive Relationships

Building and maintaining positive relationships is essential for success in your weight loss journey. By surrounding yourself with supportive and encouraging people, you can find the strength and motivation to persevere. As you continue to commit each day to the Lord, trust that He will guide and support you in cultivating positive relationships.

# DAY 10

---

## OVERCOMING TEMPTATION

Bible Verse:

_"No temptation has overtaken you except what is common to mankind. And God is faithful; he will not let you be tempted beyond what you can bear. But when you are tempted, he will also provide a way out so that you can endure it."_ – 1 Corinthians 10:13

Devotional:

Temptation is an inevitable part of any significant journey, especially when it comes to weight loss. Paul's words in 1 Corinthians 10:13 offer assurance that we are not alone in facing temptation. He reminds us that God is faithful and will not allow us to be tempted beyond what we can bear. Furthermore, He provides a way out so that we can endure it.

Understanding temptation and learning how to overcome it is crucial for long-term success. Temptation can come in many forms, such as the allure of unhealthy foods, the desire to skip workouts, or the urge to give up when progress seems slow. Recognizing these temptations and relying on God's strength to resist them is key.

Jesus' experience in the wilderness is a powerful example of overcoming temptation (Matthew 4:1-11). After fasting for forty days and nights, He was tempted by Satan. Each time, Jesus responded with Scripture, demonstrating the power of God's Word in resisting temptation. Like Jesus, we can rely on Scripture and God's faithfulness to overcome the temptations we face.

Practical Steps:

1. Identify Your Triggers:

Understanding what triggers your temptation is the first step in overcoming it. Identify the situations, emotions, or environments that lead you to make unhealthy choices.

Reflection:

- What are the common triggers for your temptations?

- How can you avoid or manage these triggers?

Example Triggers:

- Emotional stress leading to comfort eating

- Social gatherings with unhealthy food options

- Late-night cravings

2. Develop Strategies to Avoid or Overcome Temptations:

Once you know your triggers, develop practical strategies to avoid or overcome them. This may include planning ahead, seeking support, or using Scripture to strengthen your resolve.

Reflection:

- What strategies can help you resist temptation?

- How can you prepare in advance to handle tempting situations?

Example Strategies:

- Keep healthy snacks on hand to avoid unhealthy options.

- Plan your meals and workouts in advance.

- Memorize and recite Bible verses that reinforce your commitment.

3. Pray for Strength and Wisdom in Difficult Moments:

Prayer is a powerful tool in overcoming temptation. Ask God for the strength and wisdom to resist temptation and make healthy choices.

Suggested Prayer:

"Heavenly Father, I face many temptations on my weight loss journey. Please give me the strength and wisdom to resist them. Help me to rely on Your Word and Your faithfulness in difficult moments. Thank You for always providing a way out. In Jesus' name, Amen."

Reflection:

- How can regular prayer help you overcome temptation?

- What specific temptations do you need God's help with today?

Expository Bible Study:

To deepen your understanding of overcoming temptation, let's explore additional Bible passages that emphasize this theme.

1. James 1:12:

_"Blessed is the one who perseveres under trial because, having stood the test, that person will receive the crown of life that the Lord has promised to those who love him."_

Explanation:

James encourages believers to persevere under trial, promising that those who endure will receive the crown of life. This verse emphasizes the reward of enduring temptation and trials.

Application:

- Reflect on the rewards of persevering through temptation.

- Consider how enduring temptation can strengthen your faith and character.

2. Hebrews 2:18:

_"Because he himself suffered when he was tempted, he is able to help those who are being tempted."_

Explanation:

This verse reminds us that Jesus, having suffered temptation Himself, is able to help us when we are tempted. His empathy and strength are available to us in our moments of weakness.

Application:

- Reflect on how Jesus' experience with temptation can provide you with comfort and strength.

- Seek His help and guidance when you face temptation.

3. Psalm 119:11:

_"I have hidden your word in my heart that I might not sin against you."_

Explanation:

The psalmist speaks of hiding God's Word in his heart as a means of resisting sin and temptation. Memorizing and meditating on Scripture can fortify us against temptation.

Application:

- Reflect on the power of Scripture in overcoming temptation.

- Choose specific verses to memorize and meditate on to help you resist temptation.

Reflection Questions:

1. What are the common triggers for your temptations, and how can you manage them?

2. How can you prepare in advance to handle tempting situations?

3. How can prayer and Scripture help you resist temptation?

Daily Affirmation:

"I am strong in the Lord and His mighty power. With God's help, I can resist temptation and make healthy choices that honor Him."

Encouragement:

Overcoming temptation is a critical aspect of your weight loss journey. By identifying your triggers, developing strategies, and relying on God's strength, you can resist temptation and stay on track. Remember that God is faithful and will always provide a way out when you are tempted.

As you continue this 30-day journey, keep seeking God's guidance and strength. He is faithful to help you overcome temptation and make choices that honor Him. Stay committed, stay strong, and trust in the Lord's plan for your health and well-being.

Conclusion

Victory Over Temptation

Learning to overcome temptation is essential for maintaining progress in your weight loss journey. By identifying triggers, developing strategies, and relying on God's strength, you can resist temptation and stay on track. As you continue to commit each day to the Lord, trust that He will guide and support you in overcoming challenges.

# DAY 11

## GOD'S STRENGTH

Bible Verse:

_"I can do all this through him who gives me strength."_ – Philippians 4:13

Devotional:

In the journey towards achieving your weight loss goals, it's essential to recognize that you are not alone. God is your source of strength. Paul's declaration in Philippians 4:13 underscores a profound truth: our strength comes from God. When we rely on Him, we can overcome any obstacle.

This verse is often quoted for its encouragement, but it's crucial to understand its context. Paul wrote these words while imprisoned, facing hardships, yet he expressed contentment and strength through Christ. His circumstances did not define his strength; his reliance on Christ did.

Similarly, no matter what challenges you face in your weight loss journey, God's strength is available to help you persevere.

Consider the story of David and Goliath (1 Samuel 17). David, a young shepherd, faced a giant warrior with confidence, not in his own abilities, but in God's power. David's faith in God's strength allowed him to overcome an obstacle that seemed insurmountable. Like David, you can face your challenges with confidence, knowing that God's strength is with you.

Practical Steps:

1. Start Your Day with Prayer, Asking for God's Strength:

Beginning your day with prayer sets the tone for relying on God's strength. Invite God into your journey, asking for His guidance and empowerment.

Reflection:

- How can starting your day with prayer influence your actions and mindset?

- What specific areas do you need God's strength in today?

Suggested Prayer:

"Heavenly Father, I come to You this morning asking for Your strength. Help me to rely on You in every aspect of my weight loss journey. Give me the perseverance and determination to make healthy choices and overcome any obstacles. Thank You for being my source of strength. In Jesus' name, Amen."

2. Repeat Today's Verse Throughout the Day:

Meditating on Philippians 4:13 can remind you of God's constant presence and power. Repeating this verse can reinforce your reliance on Him.

Reflection:

- How can repeating this verse help you stay focused and motivated?

- What moments in your day do you feel most in need of this reminder?

Examples:

- Before meals, make mindful food choices.

- During workouts, to push through challenging moments.

- When feeling discouraged or tempted to give up.

3. Take Note of Moments When You Felt God's Strength Helping You:

Being mindful of God's strength in your daily activities can build your faith and gratitude. Reflect on how God has empowered you throughout the day.

Reflection:

- When did you feel God's strength helping you today?

- How can recognizing these moments encourage you to rely on Him more?

Examples:

- Feeling a surge of energy during a workout.

- Resisting the temptation to eat unhealthy foods.

- Finding peace and motivation in moments of prayer.

Expository Bible Study:

To deepen your understanding of relying on God's strength, let's explore additional Bible passages that emphasize this theme.

1. Isaiah 40:29-31:

_"He gives strength to the weary and increases the power of the weak. Even youths grow tired and weary, and young men stumble and fall, but those who hope in the LORD will renew their strength. They will soar on wings like eagles; they will run and not grow weary, they will walk and not be faint."_

Explanation:

Isaiah speaks of God's ability to provide strength to those who are weary. Trusting in the Lord renews our strength, enabling us to persevere and overcome challenges.

Application:

- Reflect on how hoping in the Lord can renew your strength.

- Consider how you can incorporate this promise into your daily routine.

2. 2 Corinthians 12:9-10:

_"But he said to me, 'My grace is sufficient for you, for my power is made perfect in weakness.' Therefore I will boast all the more gladly about my weaknesses, so that Christ's power may rest on me. That is why, for Christ's sake, I delight in weaknesses, in insults, in hardships, in persecutions, in difficulties. For when I am weak, then I am strong."_

Explanation:

Paul shares a profound truth about God's strength being made perfect in our weakness. Acknowledging our weaknesses allows Christ's power to work through us, turning our vulnerabilities into strengths.

Application:

- Reflect on areas of weakness where you need God's strength.

- Consider how embracing your weaknesses can allow God's power to be evident in your life.

3. Psalm 46:1:

_"God is our refuge and strength, an ever-present help in trouble."_

Explanation:

The psalmist declares God as our refuge and strength, always present to help in times of trouble. This assurance encourages us to turn to God for strength and protection.

Application:

- Reflect on how God has been a refuge and strength in your past experiences.

- Consider how you can rely on Him as your ever-present help in your current journey.

Reflection Questions:

1. How can starting your day with prayer influence your reliance on God's strength?

2. In what moments do you need to remind yourself of Philippians 4:13?

3. How can recognizing God's strength in your daily activities encourage you to trust Him more?

Daily Affirmation:

"I can do all things through Christ who gives me strength. With God's help, I can overcome any obstacle and achieve my goals."

Encouragement:

Relying on God's strength is essential for overcoming obstacles and achieving your weight loss goals. By starting your day with prayer, meditating on His Word, and recognizing His presence in your daily activities, you can draw on His strength to persevere. Remember that God is with you, empowering you to succeed.

As you continue this 30-day journey, keep seeking God's guidance and strength. He is faithful to help you overcome challenges and make choices that honor Him. Stay committed, stay strong, and trust in the Lord's plan for your health and well-being.

Conclusion

Strength from God for Every Challenge

Recognizing and relying on God's strength is crucial for success in your weight loss journey. By starting each day with prayer, meditating on His promises, and acknowledging His presence in your daily activities, you can draw on His strength to overcome obstacles. As you continue to commit each day to the Lord, trust that He will guide and support you in every step.

# DAY 12

---

## HUMILITY

Bible Verse:

_"Humble yourselves before the Lord, and he will lift you up."_ – James 4:10

Devotional:

Humility is a vital virtue in any journey of transformation, including weight loss. James 4:10 teaches us that when we humble ourselves before the Lord, He will lift us up. Humility involves recognizing our limitations and dependence on God, and understanding that we cannot achieve lasting change on our own.

In the context of weight loss, humility means acknowledging that we need God's help and the support of others. It's about letting go of pride and self-sufficiency and being open to learning, growing, and accepting assistance.

Humility allows us to be teachable, to admit when we need help, and to seek God's guidance and strength.

Consider the parable of the Pharisee and the tax collector (Luke 18:9-14). The Pharisee boasted of his righteousness, while the tax collector humbly acknowledged his sins and sought God's mercy. Jesus commended the tax collector's humility, stating that those who humble themselves will be exalted. Similarly, when we approach our weight loss journey with humility, we open ourselves to God's grace and empowerment.

Practical Steps:

1. Admit Your Weaknesses to God:

Humility begins with acknowledging our weaknesses and limitations. Bring your struggles and areas of difficulty before God in prayer.

Reflection:

- What are your weaknesses in your weight loss journey?

- How can admitting these weaknesses to God help you rely on His strength?

Suggested Prayer:

"Heavenly Father, I acknowledge my weaknesses and limitations in my weight loss journey. I need Your help and strength to overcome these challenges. Please guide me and lift me up as I humbly rely on You. In Jesus' name, Amen."

2. Seek Help and Support from Others:

Humility involves recognizing that we cannot do it alone. Be open to seeking help and support from friends, family, or professionals.

Reflection:

- Who can you turn to for support and encouragement?

- How can seeking help from others enhance your journey?

Example Actions:

- Join a weight loss support group or class.

- Ask a friend or family member to be your accountability partner.

- Consult a nutritionist or fitness trainer for guidance.

3. Be Open to Learning and Growth:

Approach your weight loss journey with a teachable spirit. Be willing to learn from your experiences, mistakes, and the wisdom of others.

Reflection:

- What new strategies or insights can you apply to your journey?

- How can being open to learning help you achieve your goals?

Example Actions:

- Read books or articles on healthy living and weight loss.

- Attend workshops or seminars on fitness and nutrition.

- Listen to podcasts or watch videos from experts in the field.

Expository Bible Study:

To deepen your understanding of humility, let's explore additional Bible passages that emphasize this theme.

1. Philippians 2:3-4:

_"Do nothing out of selfish ambition or vain conceit. Rather, in humility value others above yourselves, not looking to your own interests but each of you to the interests of the others."_

Explanation:

Paul encourages believers to act with humility, valuing others above themselves. This mindset fosters a spirit of service and consideration for others' needs.

Application:

- Reflect on how you can practice humility by valuing and serving others.

- Consider how this attitude can positively impact your relationships and journey.

2. 1 Peter 5:6-7:

_"Humble yourselves, therefore, under God's mighty hand, that he may lift you up in due time. Cast all your anxiety on him because he cares for you."_

Explanation:

Peter emphasizes the importance of humbling ourselves under God's mighty hand, trusting that He will lift us up at the right time. He also encourages us to cast our anxieties on God, knowing that He cares for us.

Application:

- Reflect on areas where you need to humble yourself and trust God's timing.

- Practice casting your anxieties on God through prayer.

3. Proverbs 22:4:

_"Humility is the fear of the LORD; its wages are riches and honor and life."_

Explanation:

This proverb highlights the rewards of humility, associating it with the fear of the Lord. Humility leads to blessings, including honor and life.

Application:

- Reflect on the blessings that come from practicing humility.

- Consider how fearing the Lord and living humbly can enrich your life.

Reflection Questions:

1. What are your weaknesses in your weight loss journey, and how can you bring them before God?

2. Who can you turn to for support and encouragement?

3. How can being open to learning and growth help you achieve your goals?

Daily Affirmation:

"I humble myself before the Lord, trusting Him to lift me up. I am open to learning and growing, and I seek His guidance and strength."

Encouragement:

Humility is a powerful virtue that opens the door to God's grace and strength. By admitting your weaknesses, seeking support, and being teachable, you can navigate your weight loss journey with wisdom and resilience. Remember that God is with you, ready to lift you up and guide you every step of the way.

As you continue this 30-day journey, keep seeking God's guidance and strength. He is faithful to help you

cultivate humility and achieve your goals. Stay committed, stay humble, and trust in the Lord's plan for your health and well-being.

Conclusion

Embracing Humility

Humility is essential for success in your weight loss journey. By admitting your weaknesses, seeking support, and being open to learning, you can rely on God's strength and guidance. As you continue to commit each day to the Lord, trust that He will lift you up and help you achieve your goals.

## JOY

Bible Verse:

_"The joy of the LORD is your strength."_ – Nehemiah 8:10

Devotional:

Joy is a powerful force that can provide strength and motivation in your weight loss journey. Nehemiah's declaration that "the joy of the LORD is your strength" reminds us that true joy comes from our relationship with God. This divine joy can uplift and sustain us, even in the face of challenges.

In the context of weight loss, joy can transform your perspective. Instead of focusing solely on the difficulties and sacrifices, joy allows you to celebrate progress, enjoy the process, and find gratitude in the journey. Joy is not dependent on circumstances but is rooted in the presence and promises of God.

Consider Paul's letter to the Philippians, written from prison, yet filled with expressions of joy and encouragement. Paul's joy was anchored in his relationship with Christ, enabling him to remain positive and hopeful despite his situation (Philippians 4:4). Similarly, you can draw strength from the joy of the Lord, allowing it to fuel your motivation and perseverance.

Practical Steps:

1. List Things That Bring You Joy:

Take time to reflect on what brings you joy. Identifying these sources of joy can help you incorporate more positivity into your daily life.

Reflection:

- What activities, people, or experiences bring you joy?

- How can you incorporate more of these joyful elements into your routine?

Example List:

- Spending time with loved ones

- Engaging in a favorite hobby or sport

- Listening to uplifting music or reading inspiring books

2. Incorporate Joyful Activities into Your Day:

Make a conscious effort to include activities that bring you joy in your daily schedule. This can boost your mood and provide motivation for your weight loss journey.

Reflection:

- How can you structure your day to include more joyful activities?

- What small changes can you make to bring more joy into your life?

Example Activities:

- Starting the day with a joyful song or prayer

- Taking breaks to do something you love, such as walking in nature or cooking a favorite meal

- Sharing moments of joy with friends and family

3. Share Your Joy with Others:

Joy is contagious. Sharing your joy with others can strengthen relationships and create a supportive, uplifting environment.

Reflection:

- How can you share your joy with others in your life?

- How can creating a joyful environment support your weight loss journey?

Suggested Prayer:

"Lord, thank You for the joy that comes from knowing You. Help me to find joy in my journey and to share that joy with others. Let Your joy be my strength and motivation each day. In Jesus' name, Amen."

Expository Bible Study:

To deepen your understanding of joy, let's explore additional Bible passages that emphasize this theme.

1. Psalm 16:11:

_"You make known to me the path of life; you will fill me with joy in your presence, with eternal pleasures at your right hand."_

Explanation:

David speaks of the joy found in God's presence and the eternal pleasures that come from a relationship with Him. This verse highlights the deep, fulfilling joy that comes from walking with God.

Application:

- Reflect on how God's presence brings joy to your life.
- Consider ways to spend more time in God's presence through prayer, worship, and reading Scripture.

2. John 15:11:

_"I have told you this so that my joy may be in you and that your joy may be complete."_

Explanation:

Jesus speaks of sharing His joy with His disciples so that their joy may be complete. This complete joy is found in abiding in Christ and living according to His teachings.

Application:

- Reflect on how abiding in Christ can bring complete joy to your life.

- Consider how you can deepen your relationship with Jesus to experience His joy more fully.

3. Romans 15:13:

_"May the God of hope fill you with all joy and peace as you trust in him, so that you may overflow with hope by the power of the Holy Spirit."_

Explanation:

Paul prays for believers to be filled with joy and peace as they trust in God, leading to an overflow of hope through the Holy Spirit. This verse connects joy with hope and trust in God.

Application:

- Reflect on how trusting in God can fill you with joy and peace.

- Consider how you can cultivate a hopeful and joyful spirit through the power of the Holy Spirit.

Reflection Questions:

1. What activities, people, or experiences bring you joy, and how can you incorporate more of these into your daily life?

2. How can sharing your joy with others create a supportive and uplifting environment?

3. How can trusting in God and abiding in Christ deepen your experience of joy?

Daily Affirmation:

"The joy of the Lord is my strength. I choose to find joy in my journey and to share that joy with others."

Encouragement:

Joy is a powerful source of strength and motivation. By identifying what brings you joy, incorporating joyful activities into your daily life, and sharing your joy with others, you can create a positive and uplifting environment for your weight loss journey. Remember that true joy comes from your relationship with God, and it can sustain you through any challenge.

As you continue this 30-day journey, keep seeking God's guidance and strength. He is faithful to help you cultivate joy and achieve your goals. Stay committed, stay joyful, and trust in the Lord's plan for your health and well-being.

Conclusion

Finding Strength in Joy

Cultivating joy is essential for success in your weight loss journey. By focusing on what brings you joy, incorporating joyful activities into your routine, and sharing your joy with others, you can draw strength and motivation from the Lord. As you continue to commit each day to the Lord, trust that He will guide and support you in finding joy in every step.

# DAY 14

---

## MINDFUL EATING

Bible Verse:

_"So whether you eat or drink or whatever you do, do it all for the glory of God."_ – 1 Corinthians 10:31

Devotional:

Mindful eating is about being fully present and aware while eating, appreciating the food, and recognizing its effects on your body. Paul's exhortation in 1 Corinthians 10:31 to do everything for the glory of God includes our eating and drinking habits. By being mindful in our approach to food, we can honor God with our bodies.

Mindful eating involves listening to your body's hunger and fullness cues, making conscious food choices, and savoring each bite. It's a practice that can help prevent overeating, improve digestion, and enhance your overall relationship with food. By incorporating mindfulness into your eating habits, you can create a more balanced and joyful approach to nourishment.

Consider Daniel's example in Daniel 1:8-16. Daniel chose to eat vegetables and drink water instead of the rich food and wine from the king's table. His mindful decision not only honored God but also led to better health. Like Daniel, we can make intentional and thoughtful choices about what and how we eat, bringing glory to God through our actions.

Practical Steps:

1. Eat Slowly and Savor Each Bite:

Taking time to eat slowly allows you to fully enjoy your food and recognize when you are satisfied, helping to prevent overeating.

Reflection:

- How can eating slowly change your relationship with food?

- What steps can you take to savor each bite and appreciate your meals?

Example Actions:

- Put your fork down between bites.

- Chew your food thoroughly.

- Focus on the flavors, textures, and aromas of your food.

2. Choose Nutritious Foods that Nourish Your Body:

Making healthy food choices is an important part of mindful eating. Focus on incorporating a variety of nutritious foods that provide the vitamins and minerals your body needs.

Reflection:

- What nutritious foods can you add to your diet?

- How can making healthy food choices help you honor God with your body?

Example Foods:

- Fresh fruits and vegetables

- Whole grains like quinoa, brown rice, and oats

- Lean proteins such as chicken, fish, and legumes

- Healthy fats from nuts, seeds, and avocados

3. Thank God for Your Meals:

Expressing gratitude for your food is a way to acknowledge God's provision and bring mindfulness to your eating habits. Take a moment to thank God before each meal.

Reflection:

- How can expressing gratitude for your food enhance your mindfulness?

- What are you thankful for in relation to your meals and nourishment?

Suggested Prayer:

"Lord, thank You for the food You have provided. Help me to eat mindfully, appreciating each bite and recognizing the nourishment it provides. May my eating habits honor You and reflect my gratitude for Your provision. In Jesus' name, Amen."

Expository Bible Study:

To deepen your understanding of mindful eating, let's explore additional Bible passages that emphasize this theme.

1. Proverbs 23:1-3:

_"When you sit to dine with a ruler, note well what is before you, and put a knife to your throat if you are given to gluttony. Do not crave his delicacies, for that food is deceptive."_

Explanation:

This proverb warns against overindulgence and encourages discernment and self-control when eating. It emphasizes the importance of being mindful about what and how much we eat.

Application:

- Reflect on how you can exercise self-control in your eating habits.

- Consider how mindfulness can help you avoid overindulgence.

2. Matthew 6:11:

_"Give us today our daily bread."_

Explanation:

Jesus' teaching in the Lord's Prayer includes a request for daily bread, symbolizing our dependence on God for our daily needs. This verse reminds us to trust God for our sustenance and to appreciate His provision each day.

Application:

- Reflect on how you can trust God to meet your daily needs.

- Practice gratitude for the food and nourishment He provides.

3. 1 Timothy 4:4-5:

_"For everything God created is good, and nothing is to be rejected if it is received with thanksgiving, because it is consecrated by the word of God and prayer."_

Explanation:

Paul teaches that everything God created is good and should be received with thanksgiving. This perspective encourages us to approach our food with gratitude and prayer, recognizing its goodness.

Application:

- Reflect on how you can receive your food with gratitude and prayer.

- Consider how mindfulness and thanksgiving can enhance your eating experience.

Reflection Questions:

1. How can eating slowly and savoring each bite change your relationship with food?

2. What nutritious foods can you incorporate into your diet to honor God with your body?

3. How can expressing gratitude for your meals enhance your mindfulness and appreciation for God's provision?

Daily Affirmation:

"I eat mindfully, savoring each bite and making healthy choices that honor God. I am grateful for the nourishment He provides."

Encouragement:

Mindful eating is a practice that can transform your relationship with food and help you honor God with your body. By eating slowly, choosing nutritious foods, and expressing gratitude, you can develop a more balanced and joyful approach to nourishment. Remember that each meal is an opportunity to bring glory to God and to appreciate His provision.

As you continue this 30-day journey, keep seeking God's guidance and strength. He is faithful to help you

cultivate mindful eating habits that honor Him. Stay committed, stay mindful, and trust in the Lord's plan for your health and well-being.

Conclusion

Honoring God Through Mindful Eating

Practicing mindful eating is essential for maintaining a healthy relationship with food and honoring God with your body. By eating slowly, making nutritious choices, and expressing gratitude, you can bring mindfulness to your meals and appreciate God's provision. As you continue to commit each day to the Lord, trust that He will guide and support you in developing mindful eating habits.

# DAY 15

---

## HOPE

Bible Verse:

_"But those who hope in the LORD will renew their strength. They will soar on wings like eagles; they will run and not grow weary, they will walk and not be faint."_ – Isaiah 40:31

Devotional:

Hope is a powerful force that can sustain and motivate us through difficult times. Isaiah 40:31 provides a beautiful promise that those who hope in the Lord will renew their strength. This verse depicts a vivid image of soaring on wings like eagles, running without growing weary, and walking without fainting, emphasizing the renewing power of hope.

In the context of your weight loss journey, hope is essential. It helps you stay focused on your goals, even when progress seems slow or challenges arise. Biblical hope is not wishful thinking but a confident expectation based on God's faithfulness. When you place your hope in the Lord, you trust in His promises and believe that He will help you achieve your goals.

Consider the story of Abraham, who hoped against hope that he would become the father of many nations as God had promised (Romans 4:18-21). Despite his and Sarah's old age, Abraham's unwavering hope in God's promise was credited to him as righteousness. Similarly, your hope in God can renew your strength and keep you pressing forward, even when circumstances seem challenging.

Practical Steps:

1. Reflect on God's Promises:

Take time to meditate on the promises of God found in Scripture. Reflecting on His promises can strengthen your hope and encourage you in your journey.

Reflection:

- What promises of God bring you hope and encouragement?

- How can you remind yourself of these promises daily?

Example Promises:

- "For I know the plans I have for you," declares the LORD, "plans to prosper you and not to harm you, plans to give you hope and a future." – Jeremiah 29:11

- "The LORD himself goes before you and will be with you; he will never leave you nor forsake you. Do not be afraid; do not be discouraged." – Deuteronomy 31:8

2. Visualize Your Goals and Trust God's Timing:

Visualization is a powerful tool. Picture yourself achieving your weight loss goals and trust that God's timing is perfect.

Reflection:

- How can visualizing your goals help you stay motivated and hopeful?

- What steps can you take today to move closer to your goals while trusting in God's timing?

Example Actions:

- Create a vision board with images and affirmations related to your goals.

- Write a letter to your future self, describing your success and thanking God for His guidance.

3. Encourage Yourself with Positive Thoughts and Affirmations:

Fill your mind with positive, hopeful thoughts and affirmations. This practice can help you maintain a hopeful attitude and keep discouragement at bay.

Reflection:

- What positive affirmations can you use to encourage yourself?

- How can focusing on positive thoughts help you stay hopeful and motivated?

Example Affirmations:

- "I am hopeful and confident in God's promises."

- "With God's help, I can achieve my goals."

- "I trust in God's perfect timing for my journey."

Expository Bible Study:

To deepen your understanding of hope, let's explore additional Bible passages that emphasize this theme.

1. Romans 15:13:

_"May the God of hope fill you with all joy and peace as you trust in him, so that you may overflow with hope by the power of the Holy Spirit."_

Explanation:

Paul prays for believers to be filled with joy and peace as they trust in God, resulting in an overflow of hope through the Holy Spirit. This verse connects hope with trust in God and the empowering work of the Holy Spirit.

Application:

- Reflect on how trusting in God can fill you with joy, peace, and hope.

- Consider how you can invite the Holy Spirit to fill you with hope each day.

2. Hebrews 6:19:

_"We have this hope as an anchor for the soul, firm and secure. It enters the inner sanctuary behind the curtain."_

Explanation:

The writer of Hebrews describes hope as an anchor for the soul, providing stability and security. This hope is rooted in the finished work of Christ, giving us confidence and assurance.

Application:

- Reflect on how hope in Christ can anchor your soul and provide stability in your journey.

- Consider how you can hold onto this hope, especially during challenging times.

3. Lamentations 3:22-24:

_"Because of the LORD's great love we are not consumed, for his compassions never fail. They are new every morning; great is your faithfulness. I say to myself, 'The LORD is my portion; therefore I will wait for him.'"_

Explanation:

Jeremiah expresses hope in God's unfailing love and compassion, which are renewed every morning. This hope is grounded in God's faithfulness and provides strength to wait on Him.

Application:

- Reflect on God's faithfulness and how His compassion is renewed every morning.

- Practice waiting on the Lord with hope and trust in His timing.

Reflection Questions:

1. What promises of God bring you hope and encouragement?

2. How can visualizing your goals and trusting in God's timing help you stay motivated?

3. What positive affirmations can you use to maintain a hopeful attitude?

Daily Affirmation:

"I place my hope in the Lord, trusting in His promises and timing. With God's help, I will achieve my goals and renew my strength."

Encouragement:

Hope in the Lord is a powerful source of strength and motivation. By reflecting on God's promises, visualizing your goals, and encouraging yourself with positive affirmations, you can maintain a hopeful attitude throughout your weight loss journey. Remember that God is faithful, and He will renew your strength as you place your hope in Him.

As you continue this 30-day journey, keep seeking God's guidance and strength. He is faithful to help you cultivate hope and achieve your goals. Stay committed, stay hopeful, and trust in the Lord's plan for your health and well-being.

Conclusion

Renewing Strength Through Hope

Cultivating hope is essential for maintaining motivation and perseverance in your weight loss journey. By focusing on God's promises, visualizing your goals, and encouraging yourself with positive affirmations, you can renew your strength and stay hopeful. As you continue to commit each day to the Lord, trust that He will guide and support you in maintaining a hopeful attitude.

# DAY 16

---

## BALANCE

Bible Verse:

_"There is a time for everything and a season for every activity under the heavens."_ – Ecclesiastes 3:1

Devotional:

Balance is a key principle in leading a healthy, fulfilling life. The writer of Ecclesiastes reminds us that there is a time for everything, emphasizing the importance of balance and proper timing in our activities. This principle is crucial in a weight loss journey, where maintaining a balanced lifestyle can lead to sustained success.

Achieving balance means managing different aspects of life effectively, including diet, exercise, rest, work, and relationships. It involves recognizing that while each component is important, no single one should dominate your life to the detriment of others. Striking the right balance helps you maintain overall well-being and prevents burnout or discouragement.

Jesus modeled a balanced life by taking time to rest and pray, even amidst His busy ministry (Mark 6:31-32). He understood the need to recharge and maintain a healthy balance between work, rest, and spiritual nourishment. Similarly, we can follow His example by incorporating balance into our daily lives.

Practical Steps:

1. Create a Balanced Schedule:

Designing a schedule that includes time for work, rest, exercise, and personal activities can help you maintain balance. This ensures that each aspect of your life receives the attention it needs.

Reflection:

- How can you create a schedule that balances different aspects of your life?

- What activities do you need to prioritize to achieve a balanced lifestyle?

Example Schedule:

- Morning: Devotion and exercise

- Daytime: Work and healthy meals

- Evening: Family time and relaxation

- Night: Rest and prayer

2. Prioritize Self-Care:

Self-care is essential for maintaining balance. It involves taking time to care for your physical, emotional, and spiritual health.

Reflection:

- What self-care practices can you incorporate into your daily routine?

- How can prioritizing self-care help you maintain balance and well-being?

Example Self-Care Practices:

- Taking breaks during work to stretch or walk

- Engaging in hobbies that bring you joy

- Spending time in prayer and meditation

3. Make Time for Family and Friends:

Relationships are an important part of a balanced life. Make time to connect with family and friends, building strong, supportive relationships.

Reflection:

- How can spending time with loved ones enhance your sense of balance?

- What steps can you take to ensure you regularly connect with family and friends?

Example Actions:

- Schedule regular family meals or outings

- Plan activities with friends that encourage healthy living

- Communicate regularly with loved ones, even if it's through phone calls or messages

Expository Bible Study:

To deepen your understanding of balance, let's explore additional Bible passages that emphasize this theme.

1. Proverbs 16:9:

_"In their hearts humans plan their course, but the LORD establishes their steps."_

Explanation:

This proverb highlights the balance between planning and trusting God to establish our steps. It encourages us to be proactive while relying on God's guidance.

Application:

- Reflect on how you can balance planning with trusting in God's guidance.

- Consider how you can seek God's direction in your daily activities.

2. Matthew 11:28-30:

_"Come to me, all you who are weary and burdened, and I will give you rest. Take my yoke upon you and learn from me, for I am gentle and humble in heart, and you will find rest for your souls. For my yoke is easy and my burden is light."_

Explanation:

Jesus invites those who are weary to find rest in Him. This passage emphasizes the importance of rest and learning from Jesus, who offers a balanced approach to life's burdens.

Application:

- Reflect on how you can find rest and balance in Jesus.

- Consider how you can learn from Jesus' example to manage life's burdens effectively.

3. Philippians 4:6-7:

_"Do not be anxious about anything, but in every situation, by prayer and petition, with thanksgiving, present your requests to God. And the peace of God, which transcends all understanding, will guard your hearts and your minds in Christ Jesus."_

Explanation:

Paul encourages believers to avoid anxiety by turning to God in prayer, leading to peace that transcends understanding. This passage highlights the balance between action (prayer) and the resulting peace from God.

Application:

- Reflect on how prayer can help you achieve balance and peace.

- Consider how you can incorporate regular prayer into your routine to manage stress and maintain balance.

Reflection Questions:

1. How can you create a balanced schedule that includes work, rest, exercise, and personal activities?

2. What self-care practices can you incorporate into your daily routine to maintain balance?

3. How can spending time with family and friends enhance your sense of balance and well-being?

Daily Affirmation:

"I strive for balance in my life, prioritizing work, rest, self-care, and relationships. With God's help, I maintain a healthy and fulfilling lifestyle."

Encouragement:

Maintaining balance is crucial for a healthy and fulfilling life. By creating a balanced schedule, prioritizing self-care, and making time for family and friends, you can achieve a harmonious lifestyle. Remember that God's guidance is essential in maintaining balance, and His presence brings peace and stability.

As you continue this 30-day journey, keep seeking God's guidance and strength. He is faithful to help you cultivate balance and achieve your goals. Stay committed, stay balanced, and trust in the Lord's plan for your health and well-being.

Conclusion

Achieving Balance in Life

Striving for balance is essential for success in your weight loss journey and overall well-being. By creating a balanced schedule, prioritizing self-care, and making time for relationships, you can maintain harmony and prevent burnout. As you continue to commit each day to the Lord, trust that He will guide and support you in achieving balance.

DAY 17

---

## SELF-LOVE AND ACCEPTANCE

Bible Verse:

_"I praise you because I am fearfully and wonderfully made; your works are wonderful, I know that full well."_ – Psalm 139:14

Devotional:

Self-love and acceptance are fundamental to any journey of transformation. Psalm 139:14 reminds us that we are fearfully and wonderfully made by God. This truth should shape how we view ourselves, recognizing our inherent worth and beauty as creations of God. Self-love is not about vanity or selfishness but about honoring God's creation—ourselves.

In the context of weight loss, self-love means treating your body with respect and kindness, recognizing that you are worthy of care and compassion. Acceptance involves acknowledging your current state without judgment and understanding that your worth is not dependent on your physical appearance. Embracing self-love and acceptance can lead to healthier habits and a more positive mindset.

Consider the story of the woman caught in adultery (John 8:1-11). Jesus did not condemn her but offered her grace and an opportunity for a new beginning. Similarly, you are invited to accept yourself as you are, knowing that you are loved and valued by God. This acceptance can empower you to make positive changes out of love for yourself rather than from a place of self-criticism.

Practical Steps:

1. Practice Positive Self-Talk:

Replace negative thoughts about yourself with positive affirmations. This practice can improve your self-esteem and encourage self-love.

Reflection:

- What negative thoughts do you need to replace with positive affirmations?

- How can positive self-talk influence your weight loss journey?

Example Affirmations:

- "I am fearfully and wonderfully made."

- "I am worthy of love and respect."

- "I choose to treat my body with kindness and care."

2. Treat Your Body with Kindness and Care:

Engage in activities that nourish and care for your body. This includes eating nutritious foods, exercising, and getting adequate rest.

Reflection:

- What activities can you incorporate to treat your body with kindness and care?

- How can these activities support your journey towards self-love and acceptance?

Example Activities:

- Preparing and enjoying healthy meals

- Participating in physical activities you enjoy

- Ensuring you get enough sleep and relaxation

3. Celebrate Your Progress and Achievements:

Acknowledge and celebrate your progress, no matter how small. This practice reinforces positive behavior and boosts your self-esteem.

Reflection:

- What recent achievements can you celebrate?

- How can celebrating your progress motivate you to continue on your journey?

Example Celebrations:

- Reward yourself with a special treat or activity

- Share your achievements with a supportive friend or family member

- Reflect on your progress in a journal and thank God for the journey

Expository Bible Study:

To deepen your understanding of self-love and acceptance, let's explore additional Bible passages that emphasize this theme.

1. 1 Corinthians 6:19-20:

_"Do you not know that your bodies are temples of the Holy Spirit, who is in you, whom you have received from God? You are not your own; you were bought at a price. Therefore honor God with your bodies."_

Explanation:

Paul emphasizes that our bodies are temples of the Holy Spirit and should be honored. This perspective encourages us to treat our bodies with respect and care.

Application:

- Reflect on how viewing your body as a temple of the Holy Spirit can influence your actions.

- Consider ways to honor God by caring for your body.

2. Ephesians 2:10:

_"For we are God's handiwork, created in Christ Jesus to do good works, which God prepared in advance for us to do."_

Explanation:

This verse reminds us that we are God's handiwork, created for a purpose. Recognizing our value and purpose can foster self-love and acceptance.

Application:

- Reflect on the truth that you are God's handiwork, created for a purpose.

- Consider how this understanding can enhance your self-worth and motivation.

3. Romans 5:8:

_"But God demonstrates his own love for us in this: While we were still sinners, Christ died for us."_

Explanation:

God's love for us is unconditional, demonstrated through Christ's sacrifice. This love is a foundation for self-acceptance, knowing that we are valued and loved by God.

Application:

- Reflect on the depth of God's love for you, regardless of your imperfections.

- Consider how this unconditional love can inspire you to love and accept yourself.

Reflection Questions:

1. What negative thoughts about yourself do you need to replace with positive affirmations?

2. How can treating your body with kindness and care support your journey towards self-love and acceptance?

3. What recent achievements can you celebrate, and how can this motivate you to continue on your journey?

Daily Affirmation:

"I am fearfully and wonderfully made by God. I choose to love and accept myself, treating my body with kindness and care."

Encouragement:

Self-love and acceptance are crucial for a healthy and fulfilling weight loss journey. By practicing positive self-talk, treating your body with kindness, and celebrating your progress, you can foster a positive and loving relationship with yourself. Remember that you are fearfully and wonderfully made, valued, and loved by God.

As you continue this 30-day journey, keep seeking God's guidance and strength. He is faithful to help you cultivate self-love and acceptance, empowering you to achieve your goals. Stay committed, stay positive, and trust in the Lord's plan for your health and well-being.

Conclusion

Embracing Self-Love and Acceptance

Cultivating self-love and acceptance is essential for maintaining a positive mindset and achieving your weight loss goals. By practicing positive self-talk, treating your body with kindness, and celebrating your progress, you can honor God's creation—yourself. As you continue to commit each day to the Lord, trust that He will guide and support you in embracing self-love and acceptance.

# DAY 18

---

## GENEROSITY

Bible Verse:

_"A generous person will prosper; whoever refreshes others will be refreshed."_ – Proverbs 11:25

Devotional:

Generosity is a powerful principle that can transform your life and the lives of those around you. Proverbs 11:25 highlights the reciprocal nature of generosity—those who refresh others will themselves be refreshed. In the context of a weight loss journey, generosity can take many forms, from sharing your experiences and knowledge to encouraging and supporting others.

Generosity isn't limited to financial giving. It includes giving your time, energy, and compassion. Being generous with your encouragement, sharing your healthy habits, or supporting someone else in their journey can create a positive and motivating environment for everyone involved. This practice aligns with the biblical principle of loving your neighbor as yourself (Mark 12:31).

Consider the story of the widow's offering (Mark 12:41-44). Despite her poverty, the widow gave all she had, demonstrating a heart of true generosity. Jesus praised her, emphasizing that generosity is measured by the heart and the sacrifice, not the amount. Similarly, your willingness to give and support others, even in small ways, can have a significant impact.

Practical Steps:

1. Encourage and Support Someone Else:

Take time to encourage and support someone else in their journey. Your words of encouragement can be a source of strength and motivation for them.

Reflection:

- Who in your life could use encouragement and support in their health journey?

- How can you offer them genuine and meaningful encouragement?

Example Actions:

- Send a thoughtful message or note of encouragement.

- Share a helpful resource or tip that has worked for you.

- Offer to be an accountability partner or workout buddy.

2. Share Your Healthy Habits:

Generosity can include sharing the healthy habits and strategies that have worked for you. This can inspire and help others on their journey.

Reflection:

- What healthy habits have made a positive impact on your life?

- How can you share these habits with others in a way that is helpful and supportive?

Example Actions:

- Post a healthy recipe or workout routine on social media.

- Invite a friend to join you for a healthy meal or exercise session.

- Share your weight loss journey and the lessons you've learned along the way.

3. Give Your Time and Energy to Help Others:

Volunteering your time and energy to support others can be a powerful act of generosity. Whether it's through community service or personal support, your efforts can make a difference.

Reflection:

- How can you use your time and energy to support others in their health and wellness goals?

- What opportunities are available for you to volunteer or get involved in your community?

Example Actions:

- Volunteer at a local charity or community event focused on health and wellness.

- Offer to help a friend or family member with meal prep or exercise planning.

- Participate in a charity walk or run to support a cause you care about.

Expository Bible Study:

To deepen your understanding of generosity, let's explore additional Bible passages that emphasize this theme.

1. 2 Corinthians 9:6-7:

_"Remember this: Whoever sows sparingly will also reap sparingly, and whoever sows generously will also reap generously. Each of you should give what you have decided in your heart to give, not reluctantly or under compulsion, for God loves a cheerful giver."_

Explanation:

Paul encourages believers to give generously and cheerfully, highlighting the principle of reaping what we sow. Generosity should come from the heart, motivated by love and joy.

Application:

- Reflect on how you can give generously and cheerfully in your life.

- Consider how your generosity can bless others and yourself.

2. Luke 6:38:

_"Give, and it will be given to you. A good measure, pressed down, shaken together, and running over, will be poured into your lap. For with the measure you use, it will be measured to you."_

Explanation:

Jesus teaches that generosity will be rewarded abundantly. The measure we use in giving will be the measure used to bless us in return.

Application:

- Reflect on how you can practice generosity in your daily life.

- Consider how God's blessings in your life can inspire you to give more.

3. Acts 20:35:

_"In everything I did, I showed you that by this kind of hard work we must help the weak, remembering the words the Lord Jesus himself said: 'It is more blessed to give than to receive.'"_

Explanation:

Paul recalls Jesus' teaching that it is more blessed to give than to receive. This principle encourages us to focus on the joy and blessing of giving.

Application:

- Reflect on the joy and fulfillment that comes from helping others.

- Consider how you can make giving a central part of your life and journey.

Reflection Questions:

1. Who in your life could use encouragement and support, and how can you offer it?

2. What healthy habits can you share with others to inspire and help them?

3. How can you use your time and energy to support others in their health and wellness goals?

Daily Affirmation:

"I am generous with my encouragement, support, and resources. As I refresh others, I am also refreshed by God's blessings."

Encouragement:

Generosity is a powerful way to bring joy and fulfillment to your life and the lives of others. By encouraging and supporting others, sharing your healthy habits, and giving your time and energy, you can create a positive and uplifting environment. Remember that your generosity will be rewarded, and you will be refreshed as you refresh others.

As you continue this 30-day journey, keep seeking God's guidance and strength. He is faithful to help you cultivate a generous spirit and achieve your goals. Stay committed, stay generous, and trust in the Lord's plan for your health and well-being.

Conclusion

The Power of Generosity

Practicing generosity is essential for a fulfilling and impactful weight loss journey. By encouraging others, sharing healthy habits, and giving your time and energy, you can create a positive environment and inspire those around you. As you continue to commit each day to the Lord, trust that He will guide and support you in cultivating a generous spirit.

# DAY 19

## FAITHFULNESS

Bible Verse:

_"Let love and faithfulness never leave you; bind them around your neck, write them on the tablet of your heart."_ — Proverbs 3:3

Devotional:

Faithfulness is a cornerstone of any successful endeavor, including your weight loss journey. Proverbs 3:3 encourages us to hold onto love and faithfulness, making them an integral part of our lives. Faithfulness involves being reliable, consistent, and steadfast in your commitments, both to yourself and to God.

In the context of weight loss, faithfulness means sticking to your plan, honoring your commitments, and persevering through challenges. It requires consistency in your actions, whether it's maintaining a healthy diet, exercising regularly, or staying focused on your goals. Faithfulness also involves trusting in God's faithfulness to support and guide you.

Consider the story of Ruth, whose faithfulness to Naomi and to God led to unexpected blessings (Ruth 1:16-17, 4:13-17). Ruth's unwavering loyalty and commitment exemplify the power of faithfulness. Similarly, your dedication and steadfastness in your weight loss journey can lead to remarkable results and personal growth.

Practical Steps:

1. Set Realistic and Achievable Goals:

Setting realistic goals helps you stay committed and motivated. Break down your larger goals into smaller, manageable steps.

Reflection:

- What are your long-term and short-term weight loss goals?

- How can setting realistic goals help you stay faithful to your plan?

Example Goals:

- Long-term: Lose 20 pounds in six months.

- Short-term: Exercise for 30 minutes, five days a week.

2. Create a Consistent Routine:

Establishing a consistent routine for your meals, exercise, and rest can help you stay faithful to your commitments. Consistency builds habits that lead to lasting change.

Reflection:

- What routine can you create to support your weight loss goals?

- How can a consistent routine help you stay on track and motivated?

Example Routine:

- Morning: Healthy breakfast and workout.

- Daytime: Balanced meals and active breaks.

- Evening: Light dinner and relaxation.

3. Trust in God's Faithfulness:

Rely on God's faithfulness to guide and support you. Trust that He will provide the strength and perseverance you need to stay committed to your journey.

Reflection:

- How can trusting in God's faithfulness encourage you in your weight loss journey?

- What specific challenges do you need to entrust to God?

Suggested Prayer:

"Lord, I commit my weight loss journey to You. Help me to remain faithful in my actions and trust in Your faithfulness. Give me the strength and perseverance to stay committed to my goals. Thank You for guiding and supporting me every step of the way. In Jesus' name, Amen."

Expository Bible Study:

To deepen your understanding of faithfulness, let's explore additional Bible passages that emphasize this theme.

1. Lamentations 3:22-23:

_"Because of the LORD's great love we are not consumed, for his compassions never fail. They are new every morning; great is your faithfulness."_

Explanation:

This passage highlights God's unfailing love and faithfulness, which are renewed every morning. Trusting in God's constant faithfulness can encourage us to remain faithful in our actions.

Application:

- Reflect on how God's faithfulness impacts your life and journey.

- Consider how you can respond to God's faithfulness with your own commitment.

2. Psalm 37:3-4:

_"Trust in the LORD and do good; dwell in the land and enjoy safe pasture. Take delight in the LORD, and he will give you the desires of your heart."_

Explanation:

The psalmist encourages trusting in the Lord and doing good, promising that delighting in God will lead to fulfillment. Faithfulness to God's ways brings blessings and satisfaction.

Application:

- Reflect on how trusting in the Lord and doing good can align your desires with God's will.

- Consider how you can take delight in the Lord in your daily actions.

3. Galatians 6:9:

_"Let us not become weary in doing good, for at the proper time we will reap a harvest if we do not give up."_

Explanation:

Paul encourages perseverance in doing good, assuring that persistence will lead to a fruitful harvest. Staying faithful, even when weary, brings eventual rewards.

Application:

- Reflect on how perseverance in doing good can lead to positive outcomes in your journey.

- Consider ways to encourage yourself to remain faithful and not give up.

Reflection Questions:

1. What are your long-term and short-term weight loss goals, and how can setting realistic goals help you stay faithful?

2. How can creating a consistent routine support your commitment to your weight loss journey?

3. How can trust in God's faithfulness encourage you to persevere through challenges?

Daily Affirmation:

"I am committed and faithful in my weight loss journey. With God's help, I persevere and trust in His faithfulness to guide and support me."

Encouragement:

Faithfulness is crucial for achieving success in your weight loss journey. By setting realistic goals, creating a consistent routine, and trusting in God's faithfulness, you can remain committed and motivated. Remember that God is with you, providing the strength and perseverance you need to stay faithful.

As you continue this 30-day journey, keep seeking God's guidance and strength. He is faithful to help you cultivate faithfulness and achieve your goals. Stay committed, stay faithful, and trust in the Lord's plan for your health and well-being.

Conclusion

The Importance of Faithfulness

Cultivating faithfulness is essential for maintaining commitment and achieving your weight loss goals. By setting realistic goals, creating a consistent routine, and trusting in God's faithfulness, you can persevere through challenges and remain steadfast in your journey. As you continue to commit each day to the Lord, trust that He will guide and support you in cultivating faithfulness.

# DAY 20

---

## GRATITUDE

Bible Verse:

_"Give thanks in all circumstances; for this is God's will for you in Christ Jesus."_ – 1 Thessalonians 5:18

Devotional:

Gratitude is a powerful and transformative practice. Paul's instruction in 1 Thessalonians 5:18 to give thanks in all circumstances highlights the importance of maintaining a grateful heart, regardless of the situations we face. Gratitude shifts our focus from what we lack to what we have, fostering contentment and joy.

In the context of your weight loss journey, practicing gratitude can enhance your motivation and resilience. It helps you appreciate your progress, celebrate small victories, and maintain a positive outlook. Gratitude reminds you of God's faithfulness and provision, encouraging you to trust Him more deeply.

Consider the story of the ten lepers in Luke 17:11-19. After being healed by Jesus, only one returned to give thanks. Jesus acknowledged his gratitude and faith, which brought additional blessings. Similarly, cultivating gratitude in your journey can open your heart to more of God's blessings and strengthen your faith.

Practical Steps:

1. Keep a Gratitude Journal:

Write down at least three things you are grateful for each day. This practice can help you focus on the positive aspects of your journey and life.

Reflection:

- What are three things you are grateful for today?

- How can maintaining a gratitude journal enhance your weight loss journey?

Example Entries:

- "I am grateful for the strength to exercise today."

- "I am thankful for the support of my friends and family."

- "I appreciate the healthy meals I can prepare and enjoy."

2. Express Gratitude to Others:

Take time to thank the people who support and encourage you. Expressing gratitude can strengthen your relationships and create a positive environment.

Reflection:

- Who has supported and encouraged you in your journey?

- How can you express your gratitude to them?

Example Actions:

- Write a thank-you note or message to someone who has helped you.

- Verbally express your appreciation to a friend or family member.

- Share your gratitude on social media to publicly acknowledge their support.

3. Thank God for Your Progress and Strength:

Regularly thank God for the progress you've made and the strength He gives you. This practice reinforces your dependence on Him and your trust in His provision.

Reflection:

- How can thanking God for your progress enhance your motivation and faith?

- What specific areas of your journey can you thank God for today?

Suggested Prayer:

"Lord, thank You for the progress I have made and the strength You give me each day. Help me to remain grateful and to recognize Your hand in every aspect of my journey. Thank You for Your faithfulness and provision. In Jesus' name, Amen."

Expository Bible Study:

To deepen your understanding of gratitude, let's explore additional Bible passages that emphasize this theme.

1. Colossians 3:15-17:

_"Let the peace of Christ rule in your hearts, since as members of one body you were called to peace. And be thankful. Let the message of Christ dwell among you richly as you teach and admonish one another with all wisdom through psalms, hymns, and songs from the Spirit, singing to God with gratitude in your hearts. And whatever you do, whether in word or deed, do it all in the name of the Lord Jesus, giving thanks to God the Father through him."_

Explanation:

Paul emphasizes the importance of letting the peace of Christ rule in our hearts and being thankful. Gratitude is an integral part of our worship and daily actions.

Application:

- Reflect on how gratitude can enhance your sense of peace and connection with God.

- Consider how you can incorporate gratitude into your daily worship and actions.

2. Philippians 4:6-7:

_"Do not be anxious about anything, but in every situation, by prayer and petition, with thanksgiving, present your requests to God. And the peace of God, which transcends all understanding, will guard your hearts and your minds in Christ Jesus."_

Explanation:

Paul encourages believers to approach God with thanksgiving in every situation, promising that God's peace will guard our hearts and minds. Gratitude is a powerful antidote to anxiety.

Application:

- Reflect on how approaching God with thanksgiving can reduce anxiety and bring peace.

- Practice incorporating thanksgiving into your prayers and petitions.

3. Psalm 100:4:

_"Enter his gates with thanksgiving and his courts with praise; give thanks to him and praise his name."_

Explanation:

This psalm highlights the importance of entering God's presence with a thankful heart. Thanksgiving and praise are integral to our worship and draw us closer to God.

Application:

- Reflect on how gratitude can deepen your relationship with God.

- Make thanksgiving and praise a regular part of your worship and daily routine.

Reflection Questions:

1. What are three things you are grateful for today, and how can maintaining a gratitude journal enhance your journey?

2. Who has supported and encouraged you, and how can you express your gratitude to them?

3. How can thank God for your progress enhance your motivation and faith?

Daily Affirmation:

"I am grateful for the progress I have made and the strength God gives me each day. I choose to focus on the positive and thank God for His blessings."

Encouragement:

Gratitude is a powerful tool that can transform your perspective and fuel your motivation. By focusing on the positive aspects of your journey and thanking God for His blessings, you can cultivate a joyful and resilient spirit. Remember that every small step forward is a reason to be thankful, and God delights in your gratitude.

As you continue this 30-day journey, keep seeking God's guidance and strength. He is faithful to help you cultivate gratitude and achieve your goals. Stay committed, stay grateful, and trust in the Lord's plan for your health and well-being.

Conclusion

Cultivating Gratitude

Practicing gratitude is essential for maintaining a positive outlook and staying motivated in your weight loss journey. By focusing on the blessings in your life and expressing thanks to God, you can develop a joyful and resilient spirit. As you continue to commit each day to the Lord, trust that He will guide and support you in cultivating a thankful heart.

# DAY 21

---

## WISDOM

Bible Verse:

_"If any of you lacks wisdom, you should ask God, who gives generously to all without finding fault, and it will be given to you."_ – James 1:5

Devotional:

Wisdom is a valuable asset in any journey, especially in one as significant as weight loss. James 1:5 encourages us to ask God for wisdom, assuring us that He gives generously to all who seek it. Wisdom helps us make informed decisions, discern the best paths, and avoid pitfalls.

In your weight loss journey, seeking God's wisdom can guide you in making healthy choices, understanding your body's needs, and developing effective strategies. Wisdom from God also provides the discernment to differentiate between temporary trends and lasting, healthy habits. By relying on God's wisdom, you can navigate challenges with confidence and grace.

Consider King Solomon, who is renowned for his wisdom. When faced with difficult decisions, Solomon sought God's wisdom, and his reign was marked by peace and prosperity (1 Kings 3:5-12). Similarly, seeking God's wisdom in your weight loss journey can lead to successful and sustainable outcomes.

Practical Steps:

1. Pray for Wisdom Daily:

Make it a habit to pray for wisdom each day. Ask God to guide your decisions and give you the understanding you need for your journey.

Reflection:

- How can praying for wisdom daily influence your decisions and actions?

- What specific areas of your weight loss journey do you need God's wisdom?

Suggested Prayer:

"Lord, I ask for Your wisdom in my weight loss journey. Guide my decisions and help me to make healthy choices. Give me the understanding and discernment I need to navigate challenges and stay on the right path. Thank You

for generously giving wisdom to those who seek it. In Jesus'
name, Amen."

2. Seek Knowledge and Understanding:

Take time to educate yourself about nutrition,
exercise, and healthy habits. Use reliable sources and seek
advice from knowledgeable individuals.

Reflection:

- What areas of nutrition and fitness do you need to
learn more about?

- How can seeking knowledge help you make
informed decisions in your weight loss journey?

Example Actions:

- Read books or articles from reputable sources on
health and wellness.

- Consult a nutritionist or fitness trainer for
personalized advice.

- Attend workshops or seminars on healthy living.

3. Apply Wisdom in Your Daily Choices:

Use the wisdom you gain to make practical, healthy
choices each day. This includes planning your meals,
exercising regularly, and avoiding unhealthy habits.

Reflection:

- How can you apply the wisdom you've gained in
your daily routine?

- What specific changes can you make to align your actions with wise decisions?

Example Actions:

- Plan balanced meals and stick to a regular eating schedule.

- Incorporate a variety of exercises into your routine to stay engaged and motivated.

- Avoid fad diets and focus on sustainable, healthy habits.

Expository Bible Study:

To deepen your understanding of wisdom, let's explore additional Bible passages that emphasize this theme.

1. Proverbs 2:6:

_"For the LORD gives wisdom; from his mouth come knowledge and understanding."_

Explanation:

This proverb highlights that wisdom, knowledge, and understanding come from the Lord. Seeking God's wisdom leads to greater insight and discernment.

Application:

- Reflect on how seeking God's wisdom can provide knowledge and understanding for your journey.

- Consider how you can regularly seek wisdom through prayer and study of God's Word.

2. Proverbs 3:5-6:

_"Trust in the LORD with all your heart and lean not on your own understanding; in all your ways submit to him, and he will make your paths straight."_

Explanation:

Trusting in the Lord and submitting to Him leads to straight paths and wise decisions. This passage emphasizes the importance of relying on God's wisdom rather than our own.

Application:

- Reflect on areas where you need to trust God more fully and submit to His guidance.

- Consider how relying on God's wisdom can lead to better decisions and outcomes.

3. Colossians 2:2-3:

_"My goal is that they may be encouraged in heart and united in love, so that they may have the full riches of complete understanding, in order that they may know the mystery of God, namely, Christ, in whom are hidden all the treasures of wisdom and knowledge."_

Explanation:

Paul speaks of the treasures of wisdom and knowledge hidden in Christ. This passage highlights the richness of understanding that comes from knowing Christ.

Application:

- Reflect on how knowing Christ can enrich your understanding and wisdom.

- Consider how you can deepen your relationship with Christ to access these treasures.

Reflection Questions:

1. How can praying for wisdom daily influence your decisions and actions in your weight loss journey?

2. What areas of nutrition and fitness do you need to learn more about to make informed decisions?

3. How can you apply the wisdom you've gained to your daily routine and choices?

Daily Affirmation:

"I seek God's wisdom in all aspects of my weight loss journey. With His guidance, I make informed and healthy choices each day."

Encouragement:

Seeking God's wisdom is essential for making informed and healthy choices in your weight loss journey. By praying for wisdom, seeking knowledge, and applying what you learn, you can navigate challenges with confidence and discernment. Remember that God generously gives wisdom to those who ask, and His guidance will lead you on the right path.

As you continue this 30-day journey, keep seeking God's guidance and strength. He is faithful to help you cultivate wisdom and achieve your goals. Stay committed, stay wise, and trust in the Lord's plan for your health and well-being.

Conclusion

The Importance of Wisdom

Cultivating wisdom is essential for making informed and healthy decisions in your weight loss journey. By praying for wisdom, seeking knowledge, and applying what you learn, you can navigate challenges with confidence and discernment. As you continue to commit each day to the Lord, trust that He will guide and support you in cultivating wisdom.

# DAY 22

---

## PERSEVERANCE

Bible Verse:

_"Blessed is the one who perseveres under trial because, having stood the test, that person will receive the crown of life that the Lord has promised to those who love him."_ – James 1:12

Devotional:

Perseverance is the ability to continue steadfastly in a course of action despite difficulties or delays in achieving success. James 1:12 highlights the blessing and reward that come to those who persevere under trials. This verse reminds us that enduring challenges with faith and determination lead to greater spiritual maturity and ultimately, the crown of life.

In your weight loss journey, perseverance is essential. There will be times when progress seems slow, when temptations arise, or when discouragement sets in. During these times, perseverance—anchored in faith and trust in God—will keep you moving forward. Remember, the journey is not just about the destination but also about the growth and resilience developed along the way.

Consider the story of Joseph, who faced numerous trials but remained faithful to God (Genesis 37-50). Despite being sold into slavery, falsely accused, and imprisoned, Joseph persevered. His faithfulness and perseverance eventually led to his rise as a leader in Egypt, saving many lives, including those of his family. Similarly, your perseverance through challenges can lead to significant personal growth and blessings.

Practical Steps:

1. Set Short-Term Goals to Stay Motivated:

Breaking down your larger weight loss goals into smaller, achievable steps can help you stay motivated and maintain your perseverance.

Reflection:

- What short-term goals can you set to stay motivated?

- How can achieving these smaller goals boost your confidence and perseverance?

Example Goals:

- Lose 2 pounds in the next two weeks.

- Complete 30 minutes of exercise five days a week for the next month.

- Prepare healthy meals for the entire week.

2. Find Encouragement in Scripture and Prayer:

Regularly read and meditate on Bible verses that encourage perseverance. Use prayer to seek God's strength and guidance.

Reflection:

- What Bible verses encourage you to persevere?

- How can incorporating these verses and prayer into your daily routine help you stay resilient?

Example Verses:

- "I can do all this through him who gives me strength." – Philippians 4:13

- "Let us not become weary in doing good, for at the proper time we will reap a harvest if we do not give up." – Galatians 6:9

Suggested Prayer:

"Lord, I seek Your strength to persevere through the challenges of my weight loss journey. Help me to remain steadfast and motivated, trusting in Your promises. Thank You for being my source of strength and encouragement. In Jesus' name, Amen."

3. Celebrate Milestones and Progress:

Acknowledge and celebrate your achievements, no matter how small. Recognizing your progress can boost your motivation and reinforce your commitment to persevere.

Reflection:

- What recent milestones or progress can you celebrate?

- How can celebrating your achievements reinforce your perseverance?

Example Celebrations:

- Treat yourself to a new workout outfit.

- Share your progress with a supportive friend or family member.

- Take a moment to thank God for your achievements in prayer.

Expository Bible Study:

To deepen your understanding of perseverance, let's explore additional Bible passages that emphasize this theme.

1. Romans 5:3-4:

_"Not only so, but we also glory in our sufferings, because we know that suffering produces perseverance; perseverance, character; and character, hope."_

Explanation:

Paul teaches that suffering and trials can produce perseverance, which in turn builds character and hope. This process leads to spiritual growth and maturity.

Application:

- Reflect on how your challenges can develop perseverance and character.

- Consider how embracing this process can lead to greater hope and faith.

2. Hebrews 12:1-2:

_"Therefore, since we are surrounded by such a great cloud of witnesses, let us throw off everything that hinders and the sin that so easily entangles. And let us run with perseverance the race marked out for us, fixing our eyes on Jesus, the pioneer and perfecter of faith. For the joy set before him, he endured the cross, scorning its shame, and sat down at the right hand of the throne of God."_

Explanation:

The writer of Hebrews encourages believers to run with perseverance, keeping their focus on Jesus. His example of enduring the cross provides the ultimate model of perseverance.

Application:

- Reflect on how focusing on Jesus can help you persevere in your journey.

- Consider ways to throw off hindrances and stay committed to your goals.

3. 2 Timothy 4:7:

_"I have fought the good fight, I have finished the race, I have kept the faith."_

Explanation:

Paul reflects on his life and ministry, emphasizing his perseverance in faith and the fulfillment of his mission. This verse highlights the importance of finishing well and remaining faithful.

Application:

- Reflect on what it means to fight the good fight and finish the race in your context.

- Consider how you can keep the faith and stay committed to your journey.

Reflection Questions:

1. What short-term goals can you set to stay motivated in your weight loss journey?

2. What Bible verses encourage you to persevere, and how can you incorporate them into your daily routine?

3. How can celebrating your achievements reinforce your perseverance and motivation?

Daily Affirmation:

"I persevere through challenges with faith and determination. With God's strength, I remain steadfast and committed to my goals."

Encouragement:

Perseverance is crucial for achieving success in your weight loss journey. By setting short-term goals, finding encouragement in Scripture and prayer, and celebrating your progress, you can maintain your motivation and resilience. Remember that God is with you, providing the strength and encouragement you need to persevere.

As you continue this 30-day journey, keep seeking God's guidance and strength. He is faithful to help you cultivate perseverance and achieve your goals. Stay committed, stay resilient, and trust in the Lord's plan for your health and well-being.

Conclusion

The Power of Perseverance

Perseverance is essential for maintaining motivation and achieving your weight loss goals. By setting short-term goals, finding encouragement in Scripture and prayer, and celebrating your progress, you can remain steadfast and committed to your journey. As you continue to commit each day to the Lord, trust that He will guide and support you in cultivating perseverance.

---

## SELF-CONTROL

Bible Verse:

_"For the Spirit God gave us does not make us timid, but gives us power, love, and self-discipline."_ – 2 Timothy 1:7

Devotional:

Self-control is an essential component of a successful weight loss journey. 2 Timothy 1:7 reminds us that God has given us a spirit of power, love, and self-discipline. Self-control enables us to make wise choices, resist temptations, and maintain our commitments. It is a fruit of the Spirit that empowers us to live a disciplined and purposeful life.

In your weight loss journey, self-control helps you to stay on track with your diet and exercise plan. It allows you to resist unhealthy cravings and make choices that align with your goals. Developing self-control is not about sheer willpower; it's about relying on the Holy Spirit to guide and strengthen you.

Consider Daniel's example in the Bible. He demonstrated self-control by choosing to eat vegetables and drink water instead of indulging in the royal food and wine (Daniel 1:8-16). His disciplined choices honored God and led to better health. Similarly, your self-control can lead to positive outcomes and honor God in your journey.

Practical Steps:

1. Identify Your Triggers and Plan Ahead:

Recognize the situations or emotions that trigger unhealthy eating habits and plan strategies to handle them.

Reflection:

- What triggers lead you to make unhealthy choices?

- How can you plan ahead to manage these triggers and maintain self-control?

Example Actions:

- Keep healthy snacks available to avoid reaching for junk food.

- Plan your meals and exercise routine for the week.

- Practice stress-relief techniques like deep breathing or taking a walk.

2. Use Scripture to Strengthen Your Resolve:

Memorize and meditate on Bible verses that reinforce the importance of self-control. Let God's Word be your guide and strength.

Reflection:

- What Bible verses encourage you to practice self-control?

- How can you incorporate these verses into your daily routine?

Example Verses:

- "I can do all this through him who gives me strength." – Philippians 4:13

- "No temptation has overtaken you except what is common to mankind. And God is faithful; he will not let you be tempted beyond what you can bear. But when you are tempted, he will also provide a way out so that you can endure it." – 1 Corinthians 10:13

3. Practice Mindfulness and Self-Awareness:

Pay attention to your thoughts and feelings, and practice mindfulness to stay present and make conscious decisions.

Reflection:

- How can practicing mindfulness help you maintain self-control?

- What techniques can you use to become more self-aware and intentional in your choices?

Example Techniques:

- Take a moment to pause and reflect before eating.

- Practice mindful eating by savoring each bite and focusing on the experience.

- Use journaling to track your progress and reflect on your journey.

Expository Bible Study:

To deepen your understanding of self-control, let's explore additional Bible passages that emphasize this theme.

1. Galatians 5:22-23:

_"But the fruit of the Spirit is love, joy, peace, forbearance, kindness, goodness, faithfulness, gentleness and self-control. Against such things, there is no law."_

Explanation:

Paul lists self-control as one of the fruits of the Spirit. This verse highlights that self-control is a result of living by the Spirit and is essential for a godly life.

Application:

- Reflect on how the Holy Spirit can help you develop self-control.

- Consider how you can cultivate the fruit of the Spirit in your daily life.

2. Proverbs 25:28:

_"Like a city whose walls are broken through is a person who lacks self-control."_

Explanation:

This proverb compares a lack of self-control to a city with broken walls, highlighting the vulnerability and chaos that result from a lack of discipline.

Application:

- Reflect on areas of your life where you need to strengthen your self-control.

- Consider how building self-control can protect and enhance your well-being.

3. Titus 2:11-12:

_"For the grace of God has appeared that offers salvation to all people. It teaches us to say 'No' to ungodliness and worldly passions, and to live self-controlled, upright and godly lives in this present age."_

Explanation:

Paul teaches that God's grace instructs us to live self-controlled, upright, and godly lives. This passage emphasizes the transformative power of grace in developing self-control.

Application:

- Reflect on how God's grace empowers you to live a self-controlled life.

- Consider how you can rely on God's grace to resist temptations and make godly choices.

Reflection Questions:

1. What triggers lead you to make unhealthy choices, and how can you plan ahead to manage these triggers?

2. What Bible verses encourage you to practice self-control, and how can you incorporate them into your daily routine?

3. How can practicing mindfulness help you maintain self-control and make intentional choices?

Daily Affirmation:

"I am empowered by the Holy Spirit to practice self-control. With God's strength, I make wise and healthy choices each day."

Encouragement:

Developing self-control is essential for achieving success in your weight loss journey. By identifying your triggers, using Scripture to strengthen your resolve, and practicing mindfulness, you can maintain self-discipline and make wise choices. Remember that the Holy Spirit empowers you to live a self-controlled and godly life.

As you continue this 30-day journey, keep seeking God's guidance and strength. He is faithful to help you cultivate self-control and achieve your goals. Stay committed, stay disciplined, and trust in the Lord's plan for your health and well-being.

Conclusion

The Importance of Self-Control

Practicing self-control is essential for maintaining discipline and achieving your weight loss goals. By identifying your triggers, using Scripture to strengthen your resolve, and practicing mindfulness, you can cultivate self-discipline and make wise choices. As you continue to commit each day to the Lord, trust that He will guide and support you in developing self-control.

# DAY 24

---

## PATIENCE

Bible Verse:

_"But let patience have her perfect work, that ye may be perfect and entire, wanting nothing."_ – James 1:4 (KJV)

Devotional:

Patience is a virtue that is essential in every aspect of life, including your weight loss journey. James 1:4 teaches us that patience, when allowed to fully develop, leads to perfection and completeness, lacking nothing. This verse underscores the importance of allowing time and perseverance to work in our favor.

In the context of weight loss, patience means understanding that progress takes time. It involves being kind to yourself, recognizing that setbacks are part of the journey, and maintaining a long-term perspective. Patience allows you to stay committed to your goals without becoming discouraged by temporary challenges or slow progress.

Consider the story of Abraham and Sarah, who waited many years for the fulfillment of God's promise of a son (Genesis 21:1-7). Despite their long wait, they witnessed God's faithfulness. Similarly, your patience and perseverance in your weight loss journey will lead to positive results and personal growth.

Practical Steps:

1. Set Realistic Expectations:

Understand that weight loss is a gradual process and set realistic expectations for your progress. Avoid comparing your journey to others.

Reflection:

- What are realistic expectations for your weight loss journey?

- How can setting realistic goals help you stay patient and motivated?

Example Goals:

- Aim to lose 1-2 pounds per week.

- Focus on non-scale victories such as increased energy or improved fitness.

2. Practice Self-Compassion:

Be kind to yourself and practice self-compassion. Recognize that setbacks are part of the journey and use them as learning opportunities.

Reflection:

- How can you show yourself compassion during setbacks?

- What positive affirmations can help you stay patient and motivated?

Example Affirmations:

- "I am patient with myself and my progress."

- "Setbacks are part of my journey, and I learn from them."

- "I celebrate my small victories and stay committed to my goals."

3. Focus on Long-Term Health:

Keep a long-term perspective on your health and wellness journey. Focus on sustainable habits rather than quick fixes.

Reflection:

- What long-term health goals do you have?

- How can focusing on long-term health help you stay patient and committed?

Example Long-Term Goals:

- Develop a balanced diet that you can maintain for life.

- Incorporate regular physical activity into your routine.

- Improve overall well-being and reduce the risk of chronic diseases.

Expository Bible Study:

To deepen your understanding of patience, let's explore additional Bible passages that emphasize this theme.

1. Romans 8:25:

_"But if we hope for what we do not see, we wait for it with patience."_

Explanation:

Paul speaks of the importance of waiting patiently for what we hope for. This verse highlights the relationship between hope and patience, encouraging us to trust in God's timing.

Application:

- Reflect on how hope can strengthen your patience.

- Consider how you can trust in God's timing for your weight loss journey.

2. Psalm 27:14:

_"Wait on the LORD: be of good courage, and he shall strengthen thine heart: wait, I say, on the LORD."_

Explanation:

The psalmist encourages us to wait on the Lord with courage, promising that He will strengthen our hearts. This verse emphasizes the importance of waiting with faith and courage.

Application:

- Reflect on how waiting on the Lord can give you strength and courage.

- Consider how you can incorporate this principle into your daily routine.

3. Isaiah 40:31:

_"But they that wait upon the LORD shall renew their strength; they shall mount up with wings as eagles; they shall run, and not be weary; and they shall walk, and not faint."_

Explanation:

Isaiah promises that those who wait on the Lord will renew their strength. This verse encourages us to trust in God's power to sustain us through challenges.

Application:

- Reflect on how waiting on the Lord can renew your strength.

- Consider how you can draw on God's strength in your weight loss journey.

Reflection Questions:

1. What are realistic expectations for your weight loss journey, and how can setting these goals help you stay patient and motivated?

2. How can you show yourself compassion during setbacks, and what positive affirmations can help you stay patient?

3. What long-term health goals do you have, and how can focusing on them help you stay patient and committed?

Daily Affirmation:

"I am patient and kind to myself. I trust in God's timing and celebrate my progress, knowing that lasting change takes time."

Encouragement:

Patience is crucial for achieving success in your weight loss journey. By setting realistic expectations, practicing self-compassion, and focusing on long-term health, you can maintain a positive and patient mindset. Remember that God's timing is perfect, and He will strengthen you as you wait.

As you continue this 30-day journey, keep seeking God's guidance and strength. He is faithful to help you cultivate patience and achieve your goals. Stay committed, stay patient, and trust in the Lord's plan for your health and well-being.

Conclusion

The Power of Patience

Practicing patience is essential for maintaining a positive and realistic mindset in your weight loss journey. By setting realistic expectations, practicing self-compassion, and focusing on long-term health, you can stay patient and committed. As you continue to commit each day to the Lord, trust that He will guide and support you in developing patience.

---

## INTEGRITY

Bible Verse:

_"The integrity of the upright guides them, but the unfaithful are destroyed by their duplicity."_ – Proverbs 11:3

Devotional:

Integrity is about being honest, transparent, and consistent in your actions and decisions. Proverbs 11:3 emphasizes the guiding power of integrity, contrasting it with the destructive nature of duplicity. Integrity ensures that your actions align with your values and commitments, providing a firm foundation for your weight loss journey.

In your weight loss journey, integrity involves being honest with yourself and others about your progress, challenges, and goals. It means staying true to your commitments, even when it's difficult, and making choices that reflect your values. Integrity helps you build trust with yourself and others, fostering a supportive environment for lasting change.

Consider the example of Job, who maintained his integrity despite immense suffering and loss (Job 2:3, 27:5). Job's unwavering commitment to righteousness and honesty is a powerful testament to the strength and importance of integrity. Similarly, your commitment to integrity in your weight loss journey can lead to personal growth and lasting success.

Practical Steps:

1. Set Clear and Honest Goals:

Establish clear and realistic goals for your weight loss journey. Be honest with yourself about what you want to achieve and why.

Reflection:

- What are your specific weight loss goals?

- How can setting clear and honest goals help you stay focused and committed?

Example Goals:

- Lose 10 pounds in three months.

- Reduce sugar intake and eat more vegetables.

- Exercise for at least 30 minutes, five times a week.

2. Track Your Progress Transparently:

Keep an honest record of your progress, including both successes and setbacks. Transparency helps you stay accountable and make informed adjustments.

Reflection:

- How can tracking your progress help you stay accountable?

- What methods can you use to track your progress honestly and effectively?

Example Methods:

- Use a journal or app to record your daily food intake and exercise.

- Regularly weigh yourself and take body measurements.

- Reflect on your emotional and mental well-being throughout the journey.

3. Stay True to Your Commitments:

Uphold the commitments you've made to yourself and others. Integrity involves following through on your promises, even when it's challenging.

Reflection:

- What commitments have you made for your weight loss journey?

- How can you ensure you stay true to these commitments?

Example Commitments:

- Attend your scheduled workouts consistently.

- Stick to your meal plan and avoid unhealthy temptations.

- Seek support from friends, family, or a community group when needed.

Expository Bible Study:

To deepen your understanding of integrity, let's explore additional Bible passages that emphasize this theme.

1. Proverbs 12:22:

_"The LORD detests lying lips, but he delights in people who are trustworthy."_

Explanation:

This proverb highlights the importance of honesty and trustworthiness. Integrity is pleasing to God and builds a foundation of trust.

Application:

- Reflect on how honesty and trustworthiness can enhance your integrity.

- Consider ways to practice honesty in your daily actions and decisions.

2. Psalm 25:21:

_"May integrity and uprightness protect me, because my hope, LORD, is in you."_

Explanation:

The psalmist prays for protection through integrity and uprightness, expressing trust in the Lord. This verse emphasizes the protective and guiding power of integrity.

Application:

- Reflect on how integrity can protect and guide you in your journey.

- Consider how trusting in the Lord can strengthen your commitment to integrity.

3. Titus 2:7-8:

_"In everything set them an example by doing what is good. In your teaching show integrity, seriousness and soundness of speech that cannot be condemned, so that those who oppose you may be ashamed because they have nothing bad to say about us."_

Explanation:

Paul instructs Titus to demonstrate integrity in all aspects of life, setting a good example for others. Integrity in actions and speech builds credibility and respect.

Application:

- Reflect on how you can set an example of integrity for others.

- Consider ways to demonstrate integrity in your words and actions.

Reflection Questions:

1. What are your specific weight loss goals, and how can setting clear and honest goals help you stay focused and committed?

2. How can tracking your progress transparently help you stay accountable?

3. What commitments have you made for your weight loss journey, and how can you ensure you stay true to them?

Daily Affirmation:

"I am committed to living with integrity in my weight loss journey. I am honest with myself and others, and I stay true to my commitments."

Encouragement:

Integrity is essential for achieving lasting success in your weight loss journey. By setting clear and honest goals, tracking your progress transparently, and staying true to your commitments, you build a foundation of trust and consistency. Remember that integrity pleases God and guides you toward your goals.

As you continue this 30-day journey, keep seeking God's guidance and strength. He is faithful to help you cultivate integrity and achieve your goals. Stay committed, stay honest, and trust in the Lord's plan for your health and well-being.

Conclusion

Living with Integrity

Practicing integrity is essential for maintaining honesty and consistency in your weight loss journey. By setting clear and honest goals, tracking your progress transparently, and staying true to your commitments, you can build a foundation of trust and success. As you continue to commit each day to the Lord, trust that He will guide and support you in cultivating integrity.

# DAY 26

---

## SURRENDER

Bible Verse:

_"Then Jesus said to his disciples, 'Whoever wants to be my disciple must deny themselves and take up their cross and follow me.'" – Matthew 16:24_

Devotional:

Surrender is a fundamental principle of the Christian faith. It involves letting go of our desires, plans, and control, and entrusting everything to God. In Matthew 16:24, Jesus calls His disciples to deny themselves, take up their cross, and follow Him. This call to surrender is not just about giving up certain behaviors or habits; it is about a complete realignment of our lives to follow God's will.

In the context of your weight loss journey, surrender means letting go of the need to control every aspect of the process and trusting in God's plan for your health and well-being. It involves acknowledging that your strength alone is not enough and that true transformation comes from aligning your efforts with God's guidance and strength. Surrendering your journey to God allows you to find peace and confidence, knowing that He is working in and through you.

Consider Jesus' own example of surrender in the Garden of Gethsemane. Facing immense anguish about His impending crucifixion, He prayed, "My Father, if it is possible, may this cup be taken from me. Yet not as I will, but as you will" (Matthew 26:39). Jesus' willingness to surrender to the Father's will, even in the face of great suffering, exemplifies the ultimate act of trust and obedience. Similarly, your journey can be marked by a profound trust in God's will, leading to lasting change and growth.

Practical Steps:

1. Reflect on Areas Where You Need to Surrender:

Take some time to reflect on areas of your life where you are holding onto control. Identify aspects of your weight loss journey where you need to surrender to God's will.

Reflection:

- Are there specific goals or expectations you have that you need to release to God?

- What fears or anxieties are preventing you from fully surrendering your journey to Him?

Example Actions:

- Write down areas where you are struggling to let go.

- Pray for God's guidance and strength to release these areas into His hands.

- Seek counsel from a trusted spiritual mentor or friend who can help you discern and surrender these areas.

2. Pray for the Courage to Let Go and Follow His Will:

Surrendering requires courage and faith. Pray for the strength to let go of your desires and trust in God's plan. Ask Him to help you follow His will, even when it's challenging.

Reflection:

- How can prayer help you find the courage to surrender your journey to God?

- What specific prayers can you offer to seek God's help in letting go?

Suggested Prayer:

"Lord, I come before You with a heart that seeks to surrender. Help me to let go of my need for control and to trust in Your perfect plan. Give me the courage to deny myself, take up my cross, and follow You. Guide my steps and strengthen my faith as I surrender my weight loss journey to You. In Jesus' name, Amen."

3. Trust God's Plan for Your Health and Well-Being:

Trust that God's plan for your health is greater than your own. He knows what is best for you and will guide you towards it. Rely on His wisdom and timing, and find peace in His provision.

Reflection:

- How can trusting God's plan bring you peace and confidence in your journey?

- What steps can you take to deepen your trust in His guidance?

Example Actions:

- Meditate on Bible verses that speak of God's faithfulness and provision.

- Share your journey with a community of believers who can support and encourage you.

- Regularly remind yourself of past instances where God has been faithful in your life.

Expository Bible Study:

To deepen your understanding of surrender, let's explore additional Bible passages that emphasize this theme.

1. Proverbs 3:5-6:

_"Trust in the LORD with all your heart and lean not on your own understanding; in all your ways submit to him, and he will make your paths straight."_

Explanation:

This passage encourages us to trust in the Lord completely and to submit our ways to Him. It highlights the importance of relying on God's wisdom rather than our own understanding.

Application:

- Reflect on how trusting in God's wisdom can guide your weight loss journey.

- Consider ways to submit your plans and actions to God's will.

2. James 4:7-8:

_"Submit yourselves, then, to God. Resist the devil, and he will flee from you. Come near to God and he will come near to you."_

Explanation:

James calls believers to submit to God and resist the devil, promising that drawing near to God will bring His presence closer. Submission involves a conscious choice to follow God and resist temptations.

Application:

- Reflect on areas where you need to resist temptation and draw nearer to God.

- Consider how submitting to God can strengthen your resolve and bring you closer to Him.

3. Psalm 37:5:

_"Commit your way to the LORD; trust in him and he will do this:"_

Explanation:

The psalmist encourages believers to commit their ways to the Lord and trust in Him, promising that God will act on their behalf. This commitment reflects a deep trust and reliance on God's guidance.

Application:

- Reflect on how committing your weight loss journey to God can bring about His action in your life.

- Consider practical ways to commit your daily efforts to His guidance and care.

Reflection Questions:

1. Are there specific goals or expectations you have that you need to release to God, and how can you do so?

2. How can prayer help you find the courage to surrender your journey to God, and what specific prayers can you offer?

3. How can trusting God's plan bring you peace and confidence in your journey, and what steps can you take to deepen your trust in His guidance?

Daily Affirmation:

"I surrender my desires and plans to God. I trust in His wisdom and guidance, knowing that His plan for my health and well-being is greater than my own."

Encouragement:

Surrender is essential for achieving lasting success and peace in your weight loss journey. By reflecting on areas where you need to let go, praying for courage, and trusting in God's plan, you can align your efforts with His will and experience true transformation. Remember that God's wisdom and guidance are far greater than our own, and He will lead you to a place of health and well-being.

As you continue this 30-day journey, keep seeking God's guidance and strength. He is faithful to help you cultivate surrender and achieve your goals. Stay committed, stay surrendered, and trust in the Lord's plan for your health and well-being.

Conclusion

The Power of Surrender

Practicing surrender is essential for aligning your weight loss journey with God's will and experiencing lasting transformation. By reflecting on areas where you need to let go, praying for courage, and trusting in God's plan, you can embrace a life of surrender and find peace and confidence in His guidance.

# DAY 27

---

## COURAGE

Bible Verse:

_"Be strong and courageous. Do not be afraid; do not be discouraged, for the LORD your God will be with you wherever you go."_ – Joshua 1:9

Devotional:

Courage is essential for overcoming the challenges and fears that arise during your weight loss journey. Joshua 1:9 encourages us to be strong and courageous, reminding us that God is with us wherever we go. This assurance gives us the strength to face obstacles with confidence and determination.

In your weight loss journey, courage means stepping out of your comfort zone, trying new things, and persevering through difficult times. It involves believing in yourself and trusting that God will provide the strength and support you need. Courage allows you to confront your fears and take bold steps toward your goals.

Consider the story of David and Goliath (1 Samuel 17). Despite being young and inexperienced, David faced the giant Goliath with courage, trusting in God's power. His bravery led to victory, demonstrating that courage, combined with faith, can overcome even the greatest challenges. Similarly, your courage, supported by faith in God, can lead to significant achievements in your weight loss journey.

Practical Steps:

1. Face Your Fears:

Identify the fears and obstacles that hold you back and confront them with courage. Acknowledge these fears and take steps to overcome them.

Reflection:

- What fears or obstacles are hindering your progress?

- How can you confront these fears with courage and faith?

Example Actions:

- Write down your fears and pray for God's strength to overcome them.

- Take small steps to face your fears, such as trying a new workout or joining a fitness class.

- Seek support from friends, family, or a community group.

2. Take Bold Steps Toward Your Goals:

Be willing to step out of your comfort zone and take bold actions that move you closer to your goals. Courage involves taking risks and trying new things.

Reflection:

- What bold steps can you take to advance your weight loss journey?

- How can taking these steps build your confidence and courage?

Example Actions:

- Sign up for a challenging fitness event, such as a 5K run or a hike.

- Try a new healthy recipe or diet plan.

- Set a new, ambitious goal and create a plan to achieve it.

3. Trust in God's Presence and Strength:

Rely on God's promise to be with you and provide the strength you need. Trusting in God's presence can give you the courage to face any challenge.

Reflection:

- How can trust in God's presence give you courage?

- What steps can you take to strengthen your trust in God's support?

Suggested Prayer:

"Lord, give me the courage to face my fears and take bold steps toward my goals. Help me to trust in Your presence and strength, knowing that You are with me every step of the way. Thank You for being my source of courage and confidence. In Jesus' name, Amen."

Expository Bible Study:

To deepen your understanding of courage, let's explore additional Bible passages that emphasize this theme.

1. Psalm 27:1:

_"The LORD is my light and my salvation—whom shall I fear? The LORD is the stronghold of my life—of whom shall I be afraid?"_

Explanation:

David expresses confidence and courage, knowing that the Lord is his light, salvation, and stronghold. This verse emphasizes the power of God's presence in overcoming fear.

Application:

- Reflect on how God's presence can dispel your fears.

- Consider ways to remind yourself of God's protection and support.

2. Isaiah 41:10:

_"So do not fear, for I am with you; do not be dismayed, for I am your God. I will strengthen you and help you; I will uphold you with my righteous right hand."_

Explanation:

God reassures His people not to fear, promising His strength, help, and support. This verse highlights God's commitment to sustaining us through challenges.

Application:

- Reflect on how God's promises can strengthen your courage.

- Consider how you can rely on God's help and support in your journey.

3. 2 Timothy 1:7:

_"For the Spirit God gave us does not make us timid, but gives us power, love, and self-discipline."_

Explanation:

Paul reminds Timothy that the Spirit of God empowers us with courage, love, and self-discipline. This verse encourages us to embrace the power and courage given by the Holy Spirit.

Application:

- Reflect on how the Holy Spirit empowers you with courage.

- Consider how you can cultivate a spirit of power, love, and self-discipline in your daily life.

Reflection Questions:

1. What fears or obstacles are hindering your progress, and how can you confront them with courage and faith?

2. What bold steps can you take to advance your weight loss journey, and how can these steps build your confidence and courage?

3. How can trusting in God's presence give you courage, and what steps can you take to strengthen your trust in God's support?

Daily Affirmation:

"I am strong and courageous. With God's presence and strength, I face my fears and take bold steps toward my goals."

Encouragement:

Courage is essential for overcoming challenges and achieving success in your weight loss journey. By facing your fears, taking bold steps, and trusting in God's presence, you can cultivate the courage needed to reach your goals. Remember that God is with you, providing the strength and support you need to be courageous.

As you continue this 30-day journey, keep seeking God's guidance and strength. He is faithful to help you

cultivate courage and achieve your goals. Stay committed, stay courageous, and trust in the Lord's plan for your health and well-being.

Conclusion

Embracing Courage

Cultivating courage is essential for maintaining confidence and resilience in your weight loss journey. By facing your fears, taking bold steps, and trusting in God's presence, you can develop the courage needed to overcome challenges and achieve your goals. As you continue to commit each day to the Lord, trust that He will guide and support you in embracing courage.

## TRUST

Bible Verse:

_"Trust in the LORD with all your heart and lean not on your own understanding; in all your ways submit to him, and he will make your paths straight."_ – Proverbs 3:5-6

Devotional:

Trust is a foundational element in any journey, including your weight loss journey. Proverbs 3:5-6 urges us to trust in the Lord with all our heart, to not rely on our own understanding, and to submit to Him in all our ways. When we place our trust in God, He guides our paths and helps us navigate the challenges we face.

In your weight loss journey, trusting in God means believing that He is with you, supporting you, and guiding you every step of the way. It involves letting go of the need to control every aspect and instead relying on His wisdom and strength. Trusting God allows you to find peace and confidence, knowing that He has a plan for your well-being and success.

Consider the story of the Israelites in the wilderness. Despite their doubts and complaints, God provided for their needs and guided them to the Promised Land (Exodus 16:4-18, Numbers 14:1-9). Trusting God's provision and guidance can similarly lead you through the uncertainties and challenges of your journey, leading to a place of health and fulfillment.

Practical Steps:

1. Surrender Your Worries to God:

Trusting in God involves surrendering your anxieties and worries to Him. Prayerfully give your concerns to God and trust that He will take care of you.

Reflection:

- What worries or anxieties do you need to surrender to God?

- How can surrendering these worries to God bring you peace and confidence?

Suggested Prayer:

"Lord, I surrender my worries and anxieties about my weight loss journey to You. Help me to trust in Your wisdom and provision. Thank You for guiding me and giving me peace. In Jesus' name, Amen."

2. Seek God's Guidance Daily:

Make it a habit to seek God's guidance through prayer, reading Scripture, and quiet reflection. Trust that He will direct your steps and provide the wisdom you need.

Reflection:

- How can seeking God's guidance daily help you trust Him more fully?

- What steps can you take to incorporate prayer and Scripture into your daily routine?

Example Actions:

- Start your day with a devotional time, reading the Bible and praying.

- Reflect on a specific Bible verse throughout the day.

- Take moments of quiet reflection to listen for God's guidance.

3. Celebrate God's Faithfulness:

Recognize and celebrate the ways God has been faithful in your journey. Reflecting on His past faithfulness can strengthen your trust in His continued guidance and provision.

Reflection:

- How has God shown His faithfulness in your weight loss journey so far?

- How can celebrating God's faithfulness strengthen your trust in Him?

Example Actions:

- Keep a journal of answered prayers and blessings.

- Share your testimonies of God's faithfulness with others.

- Thank God in prayer for His ongoing provision and guidance.

Expository Bible Study:

To deepen your understanding of trust, let's explore additional Bible passages that emphasize this theme.

1. Psalm 37:5:

_"Commit your way to the LORD; trust in him and he will do this:"_

Explanation:

This psalm encourages us to commit our ways to the Lord and trust in Him, promising that He will act on our behalf. Trusting God involves committing our plans and actions to His care.

Application:

- Reflect on how committing your ways to the Lord can enhance your trust in Him.

- Consider how you can commit your weight loss journey to God's guidance and care.

2. Jeremiah 17:7-8:

_"But blessed is the one who trusts in the LORD, whose confidence is in him. They will be like a tree planted by the water that sends out its roots by the stream. It does not fear when heat comes; its leaves are always green. It has no worries in a year of drought and never fails to bear fruit."_

Explanation:

Jeremiah describes the blessings and stability that come from trusting in the Lord. Trusting God provides security and fruitfulness, even in challenging times.

Application:

- Reflect on the stability and blessings that come from trusting in God.

- Consider how you can deepen your confidence in God's provision and care.

3. Isaiah 26:3:

_"You will keep in perfect peace those whose minds are steadfast because they trust in you."_

Explanation:

Isaiah highlights the peace that comes from trusting in God. Keeping our minds steadfast and trusting in the Lord brings a sense of calm and security.

Application:

- Reflect on how trusting in God can bring you peace.

- Practice keeping your mind steadfast on God's promises and faithfulness.

Reflection Questions:

1. What worries or anxieties do you need to surrender to God, and how can doing so bring you peace?

2. How can seeking God's guidance daily help you trust Him more fully, and what steps can you take to incorporate prayer and Scripture into your routine?

3. How has God shown His faithfulness in your journey so far, and how can celebrating this strengthen your trust in Him?

Daily Affirmation:

"I trust in the Lord with all my heart. I surrender my worries to Him and rely on His guidance and provision."

Encouragement:

Trusting in God is essential for maintaining peace and confidence in your weight loss journey. By surrendering your worries, seeking God's guidance daily, and celebrating His faithfulness, you can deepen your trust in His care and provision. Remember that God is with you, guiding your steps and providing the strength you need.

As you continue this 30-day journey, keep seeking God's guidance and strength. He is faithful to help you cultivate trust and achieve your goals. Stay committed, stay trusting, and trust in the Lord's plan for your health and well-being.

Conclusion

Trusting in God's Guidance

Cultivating trust in God is essential for maintaining peace and confidence in your weight loss journey. By surrendering your worries, seeking His guidance, and celebrating His faithfulness, you can deepen your trust in His care and provision. As you continue to commit each day to the Lord, trust that He will guide and support you in cultivating trust.

# DAY 29

---

## CONTENTMENT

Bible Verse:

_"I know what it is to be in need, and I know what it is to have plenty. I have learned the secret of being content in any and every situation, whether well fed or hungry, whether living in plenty or in want."_ – Philippians 4:12

Devotional:

Contentment is a state of satisfaction and peace regardless of external circumstances. Paul's words in Philippians 4:12 reveal that true contentment is learned and practiced, not based on material abundance or lack. This inner peace comes from trusting God and being grateful for His provision in all situations.

In your weight loss journey, contentment means appreciating your current progress while still striving towards your goals. It involves recognizing the value of each step you take and being grateful for the small victories along the way.

Contentment helps you avoid frustration and discouragement by focusing on the present moment and God's faithfulness.

Consider the Israelites in the wilderness. Despite God's continuous provision, they often grumbled and lacked contentment (Exodus 16:2-3). Their dissatisfaction led to unnecessary hardships. Similarly, cultivating contentment can prevent negative emotions and help you maintain a positive outlook on your journey.

Practical Steps:

1. Practice Gratitude:

Regularly express gratitude for your progress and the blessings in your life. Gratitude fosters contentment and helps you focus on the positive aspects of your journey.

Reflection:

- What are you grateful for in your weight loss journey?

- How can practicing gratitude enhance your contentment and peace?

Example Actions:

- Keep a gratitude journal and write down three things you are thankful for each day.

- Thank God in prayer for His provision and guidance.

- Express gratitude to those who support and encourage you.

2. Focus on the Present:

Avoid dwelling on past failures or worrying about future challenges. Focus on the present moment and the progress you are making today.

Reflection:

- How can focusing on the present moment help you cultivate contentment?

- What steps can you take to stay present and avoid distractions?

Example Actions:

- Practice mindfulness techniques, such as deep breathing or meditation.

- Set aside time each day to reflect on your current progress and achievements.

- Avoid comparing your journey to others and focus on your unique path.

3. Embrace a Positive Mindset:

Cultivate a positive mindset by affirming your worth and celebrating your achievements. A positive outlook can enhance your contentment and motivation.

Reflection:

- How can a positive mindset help you maintain contentment and motivation?

- What affirmations or practices can you incorporate to foster a positive outlook?

Example Actions:

- Use positive affirmations to remind yourself of your worth and progress.

- Surround yourself with positive influences and supportive people.

- Celebrate your achievements, no matter how small, and recognize your growth.

Expository Bible Study:

To deepen your understanding of contentment, let's explore additional Bible passages that emphasize this theme.

1. 1 Timothy 6:6-7:

_"But godliness with contentment is great gain. For we brought nothing into the world, and we can take nothing out of it."_

Explanation:

Paul emphasizes that godliness combined with contentment leads to great gain. Recognizing the temporary nature of material possessions helps us focus on spiritual growth and contentment.

Application:

- Reflect on how godliness and contentment can lead to true fulfillment.

- Consider ways to prioritize spiritual growth and contentment over material pursuits.

2. Hebrews 13:5:

_"Keep your lives free from the love of money and be content with what you have, because God has said, 'Never will I leave you; never will I forsake you.'"_

Explanation:

The writer of Hebrews encourages contentment by reminding us of God's constant presence and provision. Trusting in God's promises helps us find peace and contentment.

Application:

- Reflect on how God's presence and promises can bring you contentment.

- Consider how you can cultivate contentment by trusting in God's provision.

3. Psalm 37:4:

_"Take delight in the LORD, and he will give you the desires of your heart."_

Explanation:

This psalm teaches that finding delight in the Lord leads to fulfillment of our desires. True contentment comes from a deep relationship with God.

Application:

- Reflect on how delighting in the Lord can bring you true contentment.

- Consider ways to deepen your relationship with God and find joy in His presence.

Reflection Questions:

1. What are you grateful for in your weight loss journey, and how can practicing gratitude enhance your contentment?

2. How can focusing on the present moment help you cultivate contentment, and what steps can you take to stay present?

3. How can a positive mindset help you maintain contentment and motivation, and what affirmations or practices can you incorporate to foster a positive outlook?

Daily Affirmation:

"I am content and grateful for my progress. I trust in God's provision and delight in His presence."

Encouragement:

Cultivating contentment is essential for maintaining a positive and peaceful mindset in your weight loss journey. By practicing gratitude, focusing on the present, and embracing a positive mindset, you can find joy and satisfaction in each step of your journey. Remember that true contentment comes from trusting in God and delighting in His presence.

As you continue this 30-day journey, keep seeking God's guidance and strength. He is faithful to help you cultivate contentment and achieve your goals. Stay committed, stay content, and trust in the Lord's plan for your health and well-being.

Conclusion

Finding Peace in Contentment

Cultivating contentment is essential for maintaining a positive and peaceful mindset in your weight loss journey. By practicing gratitude, focusing on the present, and embracing a positive mindset, you can find joy and satisfaction in each step of your journey. As you continue to commit each day to the Lord, trust that He will guide and support you in cultivating contentment.

# DAY 30

---

## CONTINUED COMMITMENT

Bible Verse:

_"Therefore, my dear brothers and sisters, stand firm. Let nothing move you. Always give yourselves fully to the work of the Lord, because you know that your labor in the Lord is not in vain."_ – 1 Corinthians 15:58_

Devotional:

Congratulations on completing this 30-day journey! This is a significant milestone, but it's also a stepping stone to a lifelong commitment to health, wellness, and spiritual growth. 1 Corinthians 15:58 reminds us to stand firm, be immovable, and give ourselves fully to the work of the Lord, knowing that our labor is not in vain. This encouragement is vital as you move forward, continuing to commit your health and well-being to God.

Your weight loss journey has not been just about losing pounds; it has been about transforming your mind, body, and spirit through God's guidance. It's about developing habits that honor God and promote a healthier lifestyle. As you reflect on the past 30 days, celebrate your progress, but also look forward to the ongoing journey ahead. This commitment requires perseverance, faith, and a constant reliance on God's strength.

Consider the apostle Paul's perseverance in his ministry. Despite numerous challenges and hardships, Paul remained steadfast in his commitment to spreading the gospel and living out his faith. His dedication serves as an inspiration for us to remain committed to our health and spiritual goals, trusting that God will continue to work in us and through us.

Practical Steps:

1. Set New Goals for the Next Phase of Your Journey:

As you complete this 30-day program, take time to set new, realistic goals for the next phase of your journey. These goals will help you stay focused and motivated.

Reflection:

- What new goals can you set to continue your progress?

- How can these goals help you maintain a balanced and healthy lifestyle?

Example Goals:

- Aim to incorporate a new form of exercise into your routine, such as swimming or cycling.

- Focus on refining your diet by adding more whole foods and reducing processed foods.

- Set spiritual goals, such as deepening your prayer life or memorizing Scripture.

2. Continue to Seek God's Guidance and Strength:

Your journey does not end here. Continue to seek God's guidance and strength in every step. Make prayer, Bible study, and worship integral parts of your daily routine.

Reflection:

- How can you maintain a strong spiritual foundation as you continue your journey?

- What practices can you incorporate to ensure you stay connected to God's guidance?

Suggested Prayer:

"Lord, I thank You for guiding me through these 30 days. As I move forward, help me to set new goals and continue to seek Your guidance and strength. Keep me steadfast in my commitment to health and wellness, and may my journey honor You in every way. In Jesus' name, Amen."

3. Encourage Others by Sharing Your Testimony:

Sharing your journey and testimony can inspire and encourage others who are on a similar path. Your story can be a powerful witness to God's faithfulness and the transformative power of His guidance.

Reflection:

- How can sharing your testimony encourage others?

- What aspects of your journey might resonate with and inspire those around you?

Example Actions:

- Share your story in a church group or online community.

- Write a blog post or social media update about your experiences and progress.

- Offer to mentor or support someone who is beginning their own weight loss journey.

Expository Bible Study:

To deepen your understanding of continued commitment, let's explore additional Bible passages that emphasize this theme.

1. Philippians 3:13-14:

_"Brothers and sisters, I do not consider myself yet to have taken hold of it. But one thing I do: Forgetting what is behind and straining toward what is ahead, I press on toward the goal to win the prize for which God has called me heavenward in Christ Jesus."_

Explanation:

Paul emphasizes the importance of forgetting what is behind and pressing forward toward the goal. This passage encourages us to focus on future progress and remain committed to our calling.

Application:

- Reflect on how you can press forward with your goals, leaving past mistakes behind.

- Consider ways to maintain focus on your future progress and spiritual growth.

2. Galatians 6:9:

_"Let us not become weary in doing good, for at the proper time we will reap a harvest if we do not give up."_

Explanation:

Paul encourages perseverance, reminding us that we will reap a harvest if we do not give up. This verse underscores the importance of steadfastness in our efforts.

Application:

- Reflect on how perseverance can lead to a fruitful harvest in your health journey.

- Consider how you can stay motivated and committed, even when progress seems slow.

3. Hebrews 12:1-2:

_"Therefore, since we are surrounded by such a great cloud of witnesses, let us throw off everything that hinders and the sin that so easily entangles. And let us run with perseverance the race marked out for us, fixing our eyes on Jesus, the pioneer and perfecter of faith. For the joy set before him, he endured the cross, scorning its shame, and sat down at the right hand of the throne of God."_

Explanation:

The writer of Hebrews encourages us to run with perseverance, fixing our eyes on Jesus. This passage highlights the importance of removing hindrances and staying focused on Christ.

Application:

- Reflect on any hindrances you need to throw off to run your race effectively.

- Consider how fixing your eyes on Jesus can help you persevere in your journey.

Reflection Questions:

1. What new goals can you set to continue your progress, and how can these goals help you maintain a balanced and healthy lifestyle?

2. How can you maintain a strong spiritual foundation as you continue your journey, and what practices can you incorporate to stay connected to God's guidance?

3. How can sharing your testimony encourage others, and what aspects of your journey might resonate with and inspire those around you?

Daily Affirmation:

"I stand firm in my commitment to health and wellness. With God's guidance, I continue to seek His strength and encouragement in every step."

Encouragement:

Continued commitment is essential for maintaining progress and achieving lasting success in your weight loss journey. By setting new goals, seeking God's guidance, and encouraging others, you can remain steadfast in your efforts and inspire those around you. Remember that your labor in the Lord is not in vain, and He will continue to guide and strengthen you.

As you complete this 30-day journey, keep seeking God's guidance and strength. He is faithful to help you maintain your commitment and achieve your goals. Stay dedicated, stay encouraged, and trust in the Lord's plan for your health and well-being.

Conclusion

A Lifelong Commitment

This 30-day journey is just the beginning of a lifelong commitment to health, wellness, and spiritual growth. By setting new goals, seeking God's guidance, and sharing your testimony, you can continue to progress and inspire others. As you move forward, remember to stand firm in your commitment, trusting that your labor in the Lord is not in vain.

This completes Chapter 30: Continued Commitment. Use the principles and practical steps outlined here as you continue your lifelong journey of health, wellness, and spiritual growth. Trust in God's guidance and remain committed to honoring Him in every aspect of your life.

## A LIFELONG JOURNEY

Congratulations on completing "A 30-Day Weight Loss Bible Study." This is not the end but the beginning of a lifelong journey of health, wellness, and spiritual growth. Remember that with God, all things are possible. Keep Him at the center of your journey, and you will continue to see His blessings in your life.

Your weight loss journey has been marked by perseverance, trust, courage, and renewal. These principles are not only essential for achieving your weight loss goals but also for living a fulfilling and purposeful life. As you move forward, continue to apply the lessons you've learned and rely on God's strength and guidance.

Embrace Lifelong Habits

The habits and practices you have developed over these 30 days are building blocks for a healthy lifestyle. Continue to embrace these habits, making them a permanent part of your daily routine. Whether it's maintaining a balanced diet, staying active, practicing mindfulness, or spending time in prayer and Scripture, these habits will support your overall well-being.

Stay Connected to God

Your relationship with God is the foundation of your journey. Continue to seek His guidance, wisdom, and strength. Make time for daily devotions, prayer, and Bible study. Trust in His promises and rely on His presence to navigate the challenges and celebrate the victories that lie ahead.

Seek Support and Community

Remember that you are not alone. Surround yourself with supportive friends, family, and community members who encourage and uplift you. Share your journey with others and seek accountability partners who can help you stay on track. Being part of a community can provide motivation, support, and a sense of belonging.

Celebrate Your Progress

Take time to celebrate your progress and achievements, no matter how small. Recognize the milestones you've reached and the growth you've experienced. Celebrating your progress reinforces positive behavior and motivates you to continue moving forward.

Set New Goals

As you continue on your journey, set new goals to keep yourself motivated and challenged. Whether it's improving your fitness level, trying new healthy recipes, or deepening your spiritual walk, setting new goals helps you stay focused and driven.

Reflect and Adjust

Regularly reflect on your journey, assessing what is working well and what needs adjustment. Be open to making changes and trying new strategies as needed. Reflecting and adjusting ensures that you stay aligned with your goals and continue to make progress.

Final Prayer

Heavenly Father, we thank You for guiding us through this 30-day weight loss journey. We are grateful for the lessons learned, the progress made, and the strength gained. As we continue on this path, help us to keep You at the center of our lives. Grant us the wisdom to make healthy choices, the courage to face challenges, and the perseverance to stay committed to our goals. May our journey be a testimony of Your love, grace, and faithfulness. In Jesus' name, Amen.

Moving Forward

This journey has equipped you with tools, knowledge, and spiritual insights to continue pursuing health and wellness. Remember that each day is an opportunity to grow, learn, and improve. Stay committed to your goals, trust in God's guidance, and embrace the journey with joy and gratitude.

Congratulations on completing "A 30 Day Weight Loss Bible Study." May your journey ahead be filled with health, happiness, and spiritual growth. With God by your side, you can achieve anything. Keep moving forward, and may His blessings continue to abound in your life.

# RESOURCES FOR FURTHER STUDY

As you continue on your journey of health, wellness, and spiritual growth, here are some resources that can provide additional support, encouragement, and knowledge.

Bible Study Groups Focused on Health and Wellness

1. Faith and Fitness Bible Study Groups:

Many churches and faith-based organizations offer Bible study groups that focus on integrating health and wellness with spiritual growth. Look for local groups or online options that provide a supportive community and relevant teachings.

2. Church Health Ministries:

Some churches have health ministries that organize group activities, workshops, and seminars on topics like nutrition, exercise, and mental health, all grounded in biblical principles.

3. Christian Weight Loss Support Groups:

Joining a Christian weight loss support group can provide accountability, encouragement, and a shared sense of purpose. These groups often combine prayer, Bible study, and practical advice to help members achieve their health goals.

Books on Christian Health and Fitness

1. "The Daniel Plan" by Rick Warren, Dr. Daniel Amen, and Dr. Mark Hyman:

This book offers a comprehensive approach to healthy living based on five essential components: faith, food, fitness, focus, and friends. It provides practical tips and biblical insights to help you achieve a balanced and healthy lifestyle.

2. "Made to Crave: Satisfying Your Deepest Desire with God, Not Food" by Lysa TerKeurst:

Lysa TerKeurst shares her personal journey of finding freedom from food cravings through a deeper relationship with God. The book includes biblical principles and practical strategies for overcoming emotional eating.

3. "Fit for Faith: A Christian Woman's Guide to Total Fitness" by Kimberley Payne:

This book is designed specifically for Christian women and combines physical fitness with spiritual growth. It includes exercises, healthy eating tips, and devotionals to help you develop a holistic approach to health.

4. "Faithfully Fit: A 40-Day Devotional Plan to End the Yo-Yo Lifestyle of Chronic Dieting" by Claire Cloninger and Laura Barr:

This devotional plan helps you break free from the cycle of chronic dieting by focusing on spiritual principles and practical strategies for sustainable health.

Online Communities for Support and Encouragement

1. SparkPeople:

SparkPeople is an online community that offers a wealth of resources for weight loss, fitness, and healthy living. It includes forums, articles, meal plans, and exercise videos. You can join Christian-focused groups within the community for additional support.

2. MyFitnessPal:

MyFitnessPal is a popular app and online community that helps you track your food intake, exercise, and progress. Joining Christian-focused groups within MyFitnessPal can provide spiritual encouragement and accountability.

3. First Place for Health:

First Place for Health is a faith-based wellness program that offers online groups, resources, and support for achieving a balanced lifestyle. The program integrates Bible study, prayer, and health education.

4. Facebook Groups:

There are numerous Facebook groups dedicated to Christian health and wellness. These groups provide a platform for sharing experiences, asking for advice, and offering encouragement. Search for groups that align with your specific needs and interests.

Final Thoughts

As you continue your journey, remember that it is not just about reaching a destination but embracing a lifelong commitment to health and wellness. Use these resources to stay informed, motivated, and connected with others who share your values and goals. Keep God at the center of your journey, and trust in His guidance and strength.

Congratulations again on completing "A 30-Day Weight Loss Bible Study." May you continue to experience growth, transformation, and abundant blessings in every aspect of your life. Stay committed, stay encouraged, and keep moving forward with faith and determination.

---

## A NEW DAWN

Heavenly Father,

Thank You for guiding me through this 30-day journey. I commit my health and wellness to You. Help me to continue to seek Your strength and wisdom in every step I take. May my body, mind, and spirit be renewed and transformed by Your love. In Jesus' name, Amen.

Conclusion

This concludes "A 30 Day Weight Loss Bible Study." As you continue on your path to health and wellness, remember to lean on God for strength and guidance. May you find joy, peace, and fulfillment in every step of your journey. Keep moving forward with faith and determination, knowing that with God, all things are possible.

Congratulations, and may God bless you abundantly on your continued journey!

224

# ACKNOWLEDGMENTS

I would like to thank everyone who has supported me on this journey, including my family, friends, and spiritual mentors. Your encouragement and prayers have been invaluable.

To my family, thank you for your unwavering support and understanding. Your love and encouragement have given me the strength to persevere.

To my friends, thank you for cheering me on and holding me accountable. Your companionship and support have made this journey more enjoyable and rewarding.

To my spiritual mentors, thank you for guiding me with wisdom and faith. Your prayers and counsel have been a source of strength and inspiration.

Thank you all for being a part of this journey and for helping me grow in health, wellness, and faith.